IT'S EASIER
FOR A RICH MAN
TO ENTER HEAVEN

than for a poor man
to remain on earth

IT'S EASIER
FOR A RICH MAN
TO ENTER HEAVEN

*than for a poor man
to remain on
earth*

by
Joseph L. Felix

THOMAS NELSON PUBLISHERS
Nashville

Published in Nashville, Tennessee, by Thomas Nelson, Inc., Publishers and distributed in Canada by Lawson Falle, Ltd., Cambridge, Ontario.

Library of Congress Cataloging in Publication Data

Felix, Joseph L., 1931-
    It's easier for a rich man to enter heaven than for a poor man to remain on earth.

    1. Finance, Personal.   2. Stewardship, Christian.
I. Title.
HG179.F43   332.024   81-2035
ISBN 0-8407-5766-2   AACR2

Contents

You Can Buy Your Way Into Heaven, But It'll Take Every Cent You Have

Gustavus Adolphus was a seventeenth century Swedish king. To establish the power of his navy, he commanded that a warship, the mightiest ever known, be constructed as the navy's flagship. The vessel, built to carry five hundred persons, was fitted with powerful armaments and splendid ornamentation. Called the *Vasa* after the king's own dynasty, this magnificent ship was ordered to sail on August 10, 1628.

The Stockholm waterfront was crowded as the ship was readied to put out to sea. A two-gun salute was fired, the ship set sail—and promptly sank.

Does that story remind you of your attempts to balance the budget? Have you gone to considerable trouble to assemble facts and figures and lay out a plan for living within your income, only to find that taxes force you to live beyond your means? Have you perhaps discovered that every time you find a way to make ends meet, things come apart in the middle?

Your Investments

Andrew Tobias is the author of the recent bestseller *The Only Investment Guide You'll Ever Need*. Tobias dedicates his book: "To my broker—even if he has, from time to time, made me just that." His book is filled with good advice about what to do with your extra money—if you have any.

The book you're reading now assumes you don't have enough extra money to make Tobias' book worthwhile. The kind of investing we'll be talking about is what you do on Glory Road rather than Wall Street. We'll be dealing with investments in Frigidaire stock—like hamburger and milk. We'll also spend some time on the money you sink into the bonds of matrimony and certificates of live birth.

We'll be talking about the money God makes available to us and how we can best use it in His service. I want to share some of my personal experiences as spouse and parent of eight with you, together with some of the hints about wise spending I have picked up in recent reading.

You won't agree with everything I write, and that's fine. Some of my ideas won't fit your life. Some of the things I've found helpful won't work for you. I'll do my best, though, to make this a practical book. No one needs financial advice that won't work. In 1919 at the Versailles Peace Conference, Italy was advised to recover its commercial losses by increasing the production of its banana crop. Such advice did Italy no good since the country, in fact, has no banana crop.

The Struggle to Survive

Even with good advice, survival is a struggle for many people today. The past twenty-five years in our country have seen repeatedly unsuccessful attempts to curb inflation. Although the beginning of the '80s saw a decrease in the *rate* of inflation, prices have escalated almost two hundred percent since 1954.

That two hundred percent increase, however, has by no means been uniform across the areas in which most of us spend our money. For example, to stay one day in a hospital in 1954 cost an average of about $15. Today, the average cost is almost $150 per day, an increase of nearly one thousand percent. We have seen a five hundred percent increase in the cost of a new home. Gasoline costs have similarly increased, with a gallon of gasoline now costing at least five times as much as it did twenty-five years ago. Even the cost of mailing a first-class letter has increased by three hundred percent.

For some of us, the combination of cost-of-living raises and promotions in our careers has enabled us to keep pace. Admittedly, inflation has eroded our savings, and being in higher tax brackets has decreased the real value of our take-home pay. But on the other side of the balance sheet, the value of our homes and other possessions has increased—overall we're doing O.K.

That level of comfort certainly does not belong to all people. Senior citizens and others on fixed incomes, for example, have a pitifully difficult time keeping up with inflation. Since 1957 young couples with children also have been hit very hard since they usually have lower salaries to buy the items whose prices are rising fastest. The costs of a new home, food, and fuel are rising so fast, in fact, that they far outstrip the inflationary average.

A 1978 Roper poll reported percentages of respondents economizing against inflation in the following specific ways:

conserving electricity	72%
economizing on food	57%
economizing on clothing	54%
using or repairing items previously replaced	50%
driving at lower speeds	47%
economizing on recreation and entertainment	46%
cutting down on eating out	45%
spending more time at home	43%
using the car less often	34%

Surviving the Struggle

It was Jesus Christ who taught us how to deal with the struggle to survive. "Stop worrying, then, over questions like, 'What are we to eat, or what are we to drink, or what are we to wear?'" (Matt. 6:31). But Christ also knew how to feed five thousand people with a couple of fish and a few loaves of bread! Living on a low-salary diet, we may find it difficult to *follow* His advice. We know the best things in life are free, but it now costs $1.50 a gallon to get to them. Why, since we're going to receive a hundredfold some day, can't we have just onefold in advance?

The Lord understands. He accepts our feelings of chagrin when we go out to buy a feather pillow and find out that even down is up. He *will* provide.

One of the few Christian beliefs I have been able to apply with wholehearted consistency is my conviction that God will see that we have the money we need to do His will. It has been easy for me to follow this principle because the Lord has repeatedly shown its truth in my life. Again and again I have faced financial shortage, only to have adequate resources show up unexpectedly. The other day for instance, our insurance agent paid a visit to our home to collect an annual premium. When Hilda recorded the $140 check, it brought the checkbook balance to approximately *minus* $350. "I just don't understand your bookkeeping!" she said to me. Well, I don't really understand it either, but the next day the postman brought enough checks to cover the deficit.

I don't recommend negative balances as an economy measure, but I do testify that trust in the Lord pays dividends. His way *will* work for you.

There is, of course, no better savings or investment guide than the Scriptures. Read Matthew's account of Jesus' encounter with a rich young man who approached him asking, "Teacher, what must I do to possess everlasting life?" Christ instructed him to keep the commandments. "No problem," said the young man (it must have been easier back then). He had been following the commandments faithfully; what else should he do?

Jesus replied, "If you seek perfection, go, sell your possessions and give to the poor. You will then have treasure in heaven."

Now that's a real investment! Jesus gave the rich young ruler the opportunity to buy his way into heaven. The cost was only every cent he had! This was because his riches stood in the way of his repentance—and Jesus knew it. (So, too, no doubt, did the rich young ruler.)

But for most of the rest of us, if we are serious about our commitment to Christ and His church, we have told the Lord that what we have is His. Instead of being asked to give up all possessions, we have become His stewards, entrusted with the careful management of the material goods He has given to us.

The question is, *how* do we take care of them properly and wisely? Especially in the crunch of times like these?

That, dear friend, is what the remainder of this book will attempt to uncover. It will be a search instilled by basic biblical practicality—with some tidbits of fun and light-heartedness thrown in for good measure.

2

My Budget Is Balanced, But Now I'm Not

The inflation we have known in our lifetime carries a powerful lesson for all of us. We have seen the buying power of our financial resources ruthlessly diminished. Spiraling inflation has set us reeling as we look at what we have been able to save and realize how little it will purchase. As increases in our income fall behind the pace of inflation—or as we try to make fixed incomes stretch—we feel powerless to attend to all the demands for money that encroach upon us.

What we should recognize, however, is that this erosion of the value of our money parallels exactly the effect that passing time has on all material possessions. Eventually, homes depreciate, automobiles wear out, our most precious trinkets fall apart. Truly, you can't take it with you.

Moths, Rust, and Thieves

In counseling us to "store up heavenly treasure," Jesus gave us a guarantee beyond the capability of the best insurance company. This treasure "neither moths nor rust corrode nor thieves break in and steal" (Matt. 6:20).

Henry David Thoreau wrote, "The cost of a thing is the amount of life it requires to be exchanged for it, immediately or in the long run." Whatever we buy we pay for with some part of our lives. Often we look at price tags and blind ourselves to the fact that the real price is the amount of life effort, so many hours and minutes of our allotted time on earth, that we spent earning that sum.

If we increase our awareness of this relationship, we will be in a better position to listen to the words of Isaiah asking in astonishment, "Why spend your money for what is not bread; your wages for what fails to satisfy? . . ." (55:2). "Remember, where your treasure is, there your heart is also" (Matt. 6:21). If we work to amass earthly possessions, our hearts are bound to earth. If we aspire to heavenly things, our hearts are freed to soar.

The meaning of Christ's words becomes clearer as life reveals itself to us. If we would save our lives, we will lose them. If, on the other hand, we will give up our lives, then they will be saved.

Everything we keep for ourselves is wasted. It goes with us to our graves. Only as we give what we have to others, is it preserved beyond the limit of our years.

How we use our money both reflects and influences what we are. The miser who spends his spare moments studying his bank accounts or counting and recounting the cash he has stashed, is exhibiting his compulsive selfishness and reinforcing it.

The key concept is that we are merely stewards of the financial means the Lord has provided. As we recognize the responsibility that comes with this trust, we try to open ourselves completely to using everything we have as God would have us use it. Whether our resources are extremely limited or abundant, the *quality* of our stewardship is what counts.

God provides us with financial resources and the freedom to choose whether we will use the money for good or evil. We can spend these resources gratifying our selfish desires and acquiring things that are evil in themselves or good things which we misuse. On the other hand, money can be used to help others in a wide variety of ways. Working through

13

worthy charitable organizations, we can send money in our place to feed the hungry and clothe the naked. We can invest in the kind of life we know God wants for us and for our family. Money we save can be used as God's will for our lives reveals itself.

Concern for Others

The Christian ideal is to act on the basic concern God instills in us for helping others. Each time we use our money in service of our fellow human beings, we are giving of this concern *and* we are letting it take firmer hold on us. In time, as a popular book and movie of many years ago pointed out, this self-giving becomes "a magnificent obsession."

You can start on a small scale, while you gradually let the best that is in you come out to be of service to other people. You'll get better at it. Eventually, the commitment will take firm hold and you'll be ready to give everything you have.

Sometimes people are too literal-minded about giving God everything. One California widow, for instance, prepared a will leaving God her entire fortune. That's not quite how it is done. Turning over hoarded funds at the end of life isn't enough. We must *use* the financial gifts we've been given. Christ tells us: ". . . 'I assure you, as often as you did it for one of my least brothers, you did it for me'" (Matt. 25:40).

Our focus must be to become appreciative of everything we have received. When we begin to realize how much God has given us—to count our blessings—our hearts overflow with gratitude, and we can then turn in love to others around us.

This chain of giving often breaks down because our blessings become so much a part of us that we lose sight of their source. We take what we have as our own, as what we are owed, and fail to feel proper appreciation for the beauty God puts in each of our lives. In our complex world, it is exceedingly difficult to let God's simplicity pervade us. Yet, only in this way can we truly receive and welcome His light. Simplicity is having a single motive and purpose. It is the single-minded desire to do His will.

What happens in most of our lives is that we go on desiring and believing in many other things besides the Lord's way. We desire to be important, and we believe that it is good to be important. We covet things for ourselves, and we believe that these things will bring us happiness. We desire the satisfaction of our emotional inclinations, and we believe that we are wanting what is good. This is double-mindedness, a way of thinking which ends in a stalemate, because we are torn between two opposing desires. It cannot bring us to the light.

When we fall into the trap of acting as if what we have is really our own, we become robbers. We fail to ask continuously for His help. In time, we get out of touch with our supreme and only Source of goodness. We need God's constant renewal. Only He is good and only He can keep His gifts from withering and becoming fruitless. By maintaining an awareness of God's bounty, we'll keep ourselves in touch with His life-giving energy.

Once we succeed in wholehearted commitment to God's service, we can expect divine inflation to take over. Give the Lord 2.54 centimeters and He'll take 1.609 kilometers. He'll also take dollars, francs, marks, or pesos—but only as many as we'll be better off without.

Like the widow in the Bible, those of us who have limited resources must be willing to give all we have. Only two small coins she dropped into the collection box and yet our Lord said, "'I want you to observe that this poor widow contributed more than all the others who donated to the treasury. They gave from their surplus wealth but she gave from her want, all that she had to live on'" (Mark 12:43,44).

Responsibility

With wealth comes responsibility. ". . . More will be asked of a man to whom more has been entrusted" (Luke 12:48). Sometimes it's frightening.

A Syracuse, New York, cleaning woman was sweeping the bank floor one night when she found $40,000. After recovering from her initial shock, she decided to put the money in a paper bag and take it home with her. The following morning she immediately called the bank and requested that someone come and get the money. "I couldn't sleep all night," she said. "I was sure glad to get rid of that money."

A Chicago widow, age fifty-eight, had her purse snatched as she walked along the street one evening. The thief sprinted off with her life savings of $10,000. After a few days, a bulky envelope arrived in the mail. Opening it, she found a quantity of well-worn bills and a note from the thief reading, "I'm sorry for causing you a lot of trouble. But when I opened the purse I was just as scared as you were. I never expected to find that much money."

The thief returned all but $20.

It's a serious mistake to assume that having material wealth is necessarily contrary to God's plan. Christ has warned us about jamming the humps on our backs as we go through the needle's eye. We have to remember, though, that all things really are possible with God. When He sees fit to provide material abundance, He is merely giving us more to share with others.

Whatever the amount of our financial resources, they shouldn't be handled carelessly. Famous people are often also well-known for spending money, but few are as notoriously careless as W. C. Fields. Wherever he went he opened a bank account. Often he used fictitious names and kept no record whatsoever of his deposits. At one point, Fields told a friend in confidence that he had over seven hundred accounts and knew exactly where they were. He died without leaving this information, however, and his executors were able to locate fewer than fifty of the accounts. The bank account or safe deposit box that Fields had in Berlin is believed to have held at least $50,000. But during the bombing of the German capital, all traces of it disappeared.

Why this carelessness? Fields attributed his strange habits of storing money to a dream he had repeatedly. In the dream he saw himself stranded in a strange city without money or friends. This led him to open an account in almost every city he played in without telling anyone.

We as Christians need not feel so insecure, whether we be millionaires or on the poverty level.

Making Ends Meet

The importance of using financial resources well suggests that we should learn to be accountable. When you start a budget, you'll have to find a way to make ends meet.

"Something there is," poet Robert Frost once wrote, "that does not love a wall." Something there is, too, that does not like a budget. From deep down inside us there comes the protest that we really don't want to plan our spending. Or if we have the kind of temperament that enjoys planning, we really don't want to be constrained by the limits we set for spending in various categories.

Done correctly, budgeting is an act of humble worship. Making an inventory of our financial resources is an expression of gratitude to the Lord for the good things He has given us to use. We recognize that whatever earning power we have comes from Him and is dependent upon Him for sustenance. As we look at our needs and identify the things our money will be used for, we apply the values that are consistent with our faith and philosophy.

The first task in making ends meet is finding out how far apart they are. Technically, this is a simple, three-stage process: (1) identify available funds; (2) identify expenses; and (3) strike a balance.

First, add up all the money you'll have coming your way within a given time. Theoretically, you can budget for a day or for several years, but most of us find one month the most practical slice of time to work with.

Second, identify your fixed and flexible expenses. Fixed expenses are those that remain more or less the same from month to month, such as utilities and mortgage payments. Flexible expenses are school supplies in September and gifts for Christmas—expenses over which you have considerable control.

The third and crucial step in making ends meet is striking a balance. You must make sure that your expenses for the budgeting period are no higher than the funds available to cover them. If your first listing of income and expenses shows that your financial resources fall far short of what will be required, study the flexible expenses you have listed and see what you can trim off or move to the next month.

This three-stage process will help you make ends meet. If your best efforts at trimming do not bring income and expenses into balance, you will have to find a way to augment your income or incur a debt. In any case, this kind of financial planning will indicate in advance where you are headed and permit you to take corrective steps before serious damage occurs.

Financial Planning

The management of our financial resources should be based on the goals we are seeking to achieve. As we do our financial planning, we should start with the needs that are most obvious. Based upon these needs we can set some financial goals that are meaningful to everyone dependent on us for support.

When you figure out how your money is to be spent, it is

important that the other members of the family be actively involved. Wives not only have a right to an equal voice in how money is spent, but they also need to know the state of the family's financial affairs. Today more and more wives work outside the home and are aware of family finances, but too many widows still are caught unprepared because they were not a part of the family's planning and operation.

Children should also be given a voice in family spending plans as soon as they are old enough to begin developing a sense of monetary values. The children's perspective on family purchases—especially large items that touch their lives in a significant way—can help to balance the adult viewpoint.

Our budget, then, is merely a framework within which we plan our spending to fit the goals we have set. We need both long-term goals, like financing college or paying off the mortgage, and short-term ones such as getting the car paid off in a specified period of time. The plan we make, of course, must be one that has a reasonable chance of working.

As we set material goals for our lives we must seek the flexibility that allows us to modify them as God's will becomes clearer. Setting an objective before seeking God's guidance is unwise. Even when we sincerely seek God's will, we frequently misread what He has in mind for us. Readiness to scrap our plans if we feel called to do so is crucial.

Money Management

No matter how careful our planning, it will take considerable discipline to stick with our budget. We'll need to look for the places to tighten up, things we can easily do without. These sacrifices strengthen our moral fiber, make it possible for us to achieve our goals, and sometimes even increase our ability to help those in need.

It's not necessary to maintain a formal ledger of income and expenditures that is accurate to the last penny, but a rough accounting of the money coming and going is important. Maintain a balanced checkbook so you can tell exactly what you have at any point in time. Be sure that each check is recorded and that the balance is computed accurately.

To put our financial resources to their best possible use requires a firm resolution that we will manage our money consistently and carefully. Most of us, however frugal we might generally be, tend to follow whims more often than we should. We might set a financial objective for ourselves of saving for a much-needed automobile, but then, just after we have begun to accumulate a modest sum, yield to temptation and spend it on a luxury item. This kind of inconsistency and lack of willpower is self-destructive.

Most of our spending habits in one way or another grow out of our childhood training. Some of us develop as big spenders and generous givers. Others are more inclined to thrift. If you are inclined to overspend, you need to develop a strategy to deal with the problem. If your weakness is serious enough, consider getting the professional help of a financial planning expert or a psychologist. There is even an association in Santa Monica, California, called "Overspenders Anonymous" that provides a credit card case with padlock and key. Think that might help?

Less drastic measures of control are also available. First, understand it's not really unhealthy to feel the urge to spend. This is a better psychological condition, in fact, than always feeling the need to hold tightly to money. By simply learning to resist the urge regularly enough, you can stay within your means.

How can you tell if overspending is a problem for you? Here is a twenty-item test to help you judge whether you are spending more than you should. Just check the statements you think apply to you. It might be interesting to have other members of your family give you their opinions as well.

——— I frequently worry or feel depressed about my finances.

My Budget Is Balanced, But . . .

____ I am usually broke by payday.

____ Unusual expenses frequently throw my financial picture into chaos.

____ I don't seem to have as much money to spare as my friends have.

____ Sometimes I think I will sink into bankruptcy if I don't stop spending.

____ I am still paying for several purchases made over a year ago.

____ I sometimes have problems with an overdrawn checking account.

____ I prefer to use credit cards even when the purchase is small and I have the cash.

____ I no longer seem to be able to put money into savings.

____ I sometimes juggle payments from one month to the next to satisfy my creditors.

____ When the statements from my creditors come at income tax time, I am surprised at how high the interest figure is.

____ My family and friends joke with me about my champagne tastes and beer budget.

____ I seem to have little willpower when faced with a purchasing decision.

____ I view shopping as a kind of recreation.

____ I sometimes feel in a low mood before and after shopping, but not while I'm doing it.

____ Sometimes I wonder why I made a particular purchase.

____ I sometimes give away things I've bought because I don't really need or want them.

____ On payday I have to hurry to the bank before the checks I've written come in.

____ When I clean up a debt it's a good feeling to be free to spend more.

_____ My credit cards are usually at the maximum credit line available to me.

Draw your conclusions about your spending with the following key: 0 to 6—little or no problem with overspending; 7 to 13—try tightening up before overspending becomes serious; 14 to 20—you really need help in slowing down your expenditures.

3

My Butcher Advertises "Meat to Fit Your Pocketbook"—And It Does!

Whoever thought meatloaf would make us nostalgic? Remember how we used to look down on hamburger? Now that our freezers are stocked with little more than applesauce, we realize we didn't know how well off we were. We gave those turkey giblets to the dog with such abandon. The fat was trimmed off every cut of meat and mixed with other table scraps for the hound to enjoy.

Now a piece of fatty meat creates a feeling of nostalgia for the old days. The high cost of meat is separating people into two classes: those with large incomes and vegetarians. It makes you wish they'd find a way to take the preservatives out of our food and put them into our money.

When we give thanks at mealtime these days, it's for being able to afford another one. Keeping enough food on the table has always been an important budgetary concern, though, even in the good old days when women put food into cans instead of just taking it out. We've always worried too much about where our meals are coming from.

Jesus told us not to waste time this way: "I warn you, then: do not worry about your livelihood, what you are to eat or drink or use for clothing. . . . Look at the birds in the sky. They do not sow or reap, they gather nothing into barns; yet your heavenly Father feeds them. Are you not more important than they?" (Matt. 6:25,26).

Importance of Food

This scripture doesn't mean not to economize on food. Eating is important to life and health. And in these days when you can lose your shirt not only in the stock market but in the supermarket as well, you do have to be careful. Supermarkets are a convenience that permit you to go broke all in one store. They now have high-speed grocery carts that do over a hundred dollars an hour, and there is no easier way to break a hundred-dollar bill than to drop it on a supermarket checkout counter.

The importance of the food we eat in determining the condition of our health and the development of our body has popularized the saying, "You are what you eat." Health food advocates abound. There are people in the world, though, who take this statement much more literally. They believe a person actually acquires the characteristics of whatever animal he consumes. Among the Malays of Singapore, for instance, the flesh of a tiger is extremely precious, since by eating it the people believe they will acquire the courage, strength, and wisdom of that animal.

We think such ideas are strange. But from the point of view of some of the poorer nations in the world it is just as strange that a country like ours pays farmers not to grow food and can't find better ways of sharing what we have. While a third of the world is dieting, the other two-thirds are starving.

Perhaps we should consider the possibility that despite their terrible suffering, many of the starving peoples of the world are better off than we are. Listen to Mary, the mother of Jesus, tell her cousin Elizabeth of God's response to them: "The hungry he has given every good thing, while the rich he has sent empty away" (Luke 1:53). Then reread Christ's parable of Lazarus and the rich man (see Luke 16:19–31).

We can be very sure that the Lord blesses our every effort to save money on what we eat in order to share more generously with our fellow human beings. The single most effective way of economizing on food is by controlling our appetites and monitoring our diet, so that our eating habits better serve their basic purpose of maintaining health and vitality.

Moderation in Eating

There's a marked similarity between some of the weight-control advice of recent years and the long-standing guidance of theologians. To show you what I mean, here are four violations of "the rules of sobriety," paraphrased from an old text on moral theology:

1. Eating between meals just to indulge our greed
2. Seeking delicacies or daintily prepared meats
3. Gorging oneself beyond appetite or need
4. Eating with greed as certain animals do.

You've heard of frozen meats, frozen vegetables, and frozen desserts. But when a Rovno, Russia, storekeeper opened his cold storage room one morning, he found a quick-frozen thief. The burglar was curled up among the sausages and hams. He had climbed into the shop during the night and somehow had fallen asleep in the meat locker. He was chilled but thankful when the police awoke him several hours later.

Few of us are rewarded so uniquely for our covetousness in regard to food. But just imagine the crisp, rich aroma of bacon frying in a skillet. Feel the dull ache in the pit of your stomach signaling your body's need for nourishment. Picture your plate piled high with hot cakes topped with butter and syrup. It's hard to resist!

All of us who enjoy good food are sometimes guilty of overeating. Admittedly most of us would not go as far as the eighteenth century Englishman named Jack Biggers, who carried things to a ridiculous extreme and paid with his life. Within an hour, he consumed all but a few bites of a meal consisting of six pounds of bacon, a huge green salad, twelve dumplings, a loaf of bread, and a gallon of beer. Just before he finished, he suffered a fatal attack of apoplexy.

Even though we have more self-restraint than this poor man, most of us honestly eat too well. Our health is affected, and even more importantly we ignore the fact that sharing with others involves freely giving up comforts that we enjoy. Merely accepting the ordinary deprivations that life brings is hard for most of us; to give up something we enjoy when we have the power to hold on to it seldom even occurs to us.

The Pleasure Drive

An instinctive tendency of our animal nature is to move toward pleasure and away from discomfort. Animals in the wild follow the same drive, though it is easier to observe among our pets or animals in captivity. In Sydney, Australia, a man found two flat tires on his car on two successive hot summer days. After looking carefully but finding no punctures, he decided that pranksters must be responsible. On the third day he watched the vehicle closely. Soon he discovered Luv, his pet cockatoo, using his beak to press the valve down while he flapped ecstatically in the cool air gushing from the tire.

Then there was the family in Leeds, England, who were puzzled by a sudden increase in the electric bill. The sixteen-year-old daughter solved this mystery when she came home early from school one day and found the family dog, Jeremy, switching on the electric heater with his paw so that he could snooze in comfort when he was alone in the house.

Like Luv and Jeremy, we humans instinctively seek comfort rather than misery; ease rather than hardship. In order to gain control of our appetites and passions, we need to start giving up some of the creature comforts we relish.

"All right, suppose I start taking my coffee without sugar. What good will this do?"

26

"Meat to Fit Your Pocketbook"

Granted, such a feat is not likely to shake the earth, but the *attitude* of self-control will lead to far more good than you can imagine. At the very least, it will enable you to understand more fully the self-denial of Christ.

It's a very human tendency when we are enjoying a good meal, celebrating a special social event, or delighting in making love, to become totally absorbed in the pleasure of the moment and act as if this delight will last forever. Yet we know that all the good things of this earth must be held in a loose grasp. Even while rejoicing over our ability to enjoy good food, we should be aware that the hunger that permits this enjoyment is a sign of our mortality. We must eat to live. But even with the best of care, our bodies will eventually wear out. All of us, from truck stop patrons to gourmets, are bound for the same demise.

Let us look upon whatever we possess as a loan. As soon as we try to make these good things our own, we misuse them. In time, even the more permanent riches of this life slip away from us. All good things—all the blessings and happy experiences of our lives—are only poor reflections of the perfect and eternal goodness we will experience in our union with God. The treasure that is given to us for a time and then taken back is deposited for us in the infinity of His love. When we have been freed of the limitations of our finite, temporary nature, we will experience all goodness in its perfect form. The transformation will be wonderful and complete.

The Need for Self-Discipline

To use our appetites in God's service, we need to understand them. Our instincts for food, affection, and pleasure should be perceived as forces built into us by God. He created our appetites as part of us, intending that we should want comforts and pleasures. All our appetites, though, are actually rooted in one fundamental desire—our need for

God. Our desires are constant reminders that we are not self-sufficient. Even if all you want is a dill pickle à la mode, that small craving will keep you aware that you are incomplete.

Christ has told us that unless we repent we will perish. He has also promised us that if we take up our cross and follow Him, we will know an unimaginably blessed eternity, in which He gives us back a hundredfold everything we have given up.

A positive view of repentance as self-renunciation to make room for the love of God has remarkable drawing power. Many of us are discouraged from acts of self-denial because we see them from a totally inaccurate angle. Or when we hear the word *discipline* we think immediately of disagreeable, external regulations to impose upon ourselves. Understandably, we draw back. If we can learn to see repentance and self-control from the true perspective, we will be spurred on to gather our whole selves together and turn completely toward God.

Successful use of our appetites, then, is not first and foremost a matter of suppressing the unruly, a painful fight against our baser nature. The real secret of success lies in healing and wholeness, bringing our natures into accord with God. As we allow God His rightful place as the ruler of our appetites, our desires are focused rightly. Increasingly, what pleasure we seek is the pleasure He wants us to have. Little by little, we develop a detachment from this world that changes our obsessive craving for attractive things we can't have.

Dieting

God's healing even helps us do without all those sweet delicacies that spend two minutes on the tongue, two hours in the tummy, and the rest of our lives on the torso. We all know how quickly cheesecake turns into pound cake. Dieting is the penalty we have to pay for going over the feed limit.

"I feel fit as a fiddle," one woman said, "but I'm shaped more like a cello." Her husband had a similar problem: "My doctor put me on a seven-day diet, but I ate the whole thing in one meal." Personally, I'm a light eater; as soon as it gets light I start eating.

But Hilda and I have begun to participate in the Weight Watchers program. Each of us has managed to shed about twenty unneeded pounds. This benefit almost makes it worth the trouble of putting up with a diet based on such incredible foods as dandelion greens and nasturtium leaves. "But Mom, you threw away a whole week's food when you weeded the lawn!"

Even more challenging than staying on the diet, though, is attending the incredibly inane lectures (I suppose it might help if there were at least one other male in attendance). For some reason I get exasperated listening to a lecturer extol the delectable quality of barbecued tuna. Every time I leave the hall, I am reminded of a cartoon in which Andy Capp sees two ladies leaving a health and beauty club. He remarks: "They must be two of the healthy ones!"

What we can eat has become a problem in our world—and not just when food is scarce. The tremendous popularity of books on how to save your life (or save your figure) by dieting gives ample evidence of this.

Back around 1960 Dr. Herman Taller wrote a book called *Calories Don't Count.* The method of weight loss Taller suggested was to eat as much as you wanted as long as the diet maintained a balance of two-thirds fats, one-third proteins, and almost no carbohydrates. In addition, Taller recommended a dietary supplement called CDC tablets, which he said were the key to maintaining health while shedding weight.

In 1963 the Federal Trade Commission barred Taller from continuing to distribute his book. By that time the popularity of his unrestricted diet had brought him considerable fame and fortune. For obvious reasons, people with weight problems were enthusiastic about being able to consume as many as 5000 calories a day and still lose weight.

But the FTC insisted that calories *do* count, and that low-carbohydrate diets were generally not sufficient for most people to lose weight. Furthermore, the Food and Drug Administration found that the CDC tablets contained nothing but safflower oil. There was nothing in them to contribute to weight loss or maintenance of health.

It seems that Taller had an agreement with the pharmaceutical company that made CDC tablets through which the author got a percentage of the profits for all tablets sold. Both the company and Taller were convicted of mail fraud and violations of the Food, Drug, and Cosmetics Act.

Feeding Our Families

Being conned we can do without. It's hard enough just keeping up, as you know if you've been shopping lately. The toddler had it right when he said, "Mommy went to the supermarkup." These days a bargain at the supermarket is anything that's overpriced less than it should be.

On the other hand, if it weren't for inflation, many of us wouldn't know beans—or any of the other less expensive foods that are often the best for us. One husband reported that his wife has found a very easy way to help him lose weight: She keeps the supermarket cash register slip taped to the refrigerator door.

Some mothers of large families have found that their limited food budgets are a real asset in helping kids maintain better health. If you don't have the money to buy a lot of sugary snacks, kids can learn to do without them. Dental cavities will be fewer, weight problems will be lessened, and tendencies toward hyperactive behavior will often be minimized. Bread seldom gets moldy in a big family.

"Meat to Fit Your Pocketbook"

If denied an ice-cream cone just before dinner, the school-aged boy will usually complain that he never gets what he wants. But food is one avenue in which parents can teach their children good judgment, self-control—and show how much they love them. Our heavenly Father teaches us in much the same way. He is infinitely more solicitous for our welfare than even the most conscientious earthly parent. And sometimes He teaches us through strict diets—tight budgets or difficult circumstances. But He watches over our lives with a tender, loving care that inventories the very hairs of our head—even as they fall out in profusion.

Not only that. God is also in complete control of things. Just as He sees everything that takes place in our lives, so also He is able to cause things to happen or prevent them, according to what He knows is best for us. In all of this, He follows a plan that is absolutely flawless.

We can compare the plan of God's providence with the recipe for baking a cake. The recipe might call for shortening, flour, baking powder, and bitter chocolate. None of these ingredients tastes very good by itself. When they are combined in the cake, however, the product is a delight to our taste buds. So also with the many events that happen in our lives. Any one of them could be as distasteful as a spoonful of raw flour. When God completes the recipe, however, we can have perfect confidence that the end result will be infinitely more pleasant than any Duncan Hines masterpiece.

Striving to realize these truths more vividly makes us able to accept God's will for us, even when it runs contrary to our plan. Our constant complaining gradually is transformed into acts of submission, prayers for strength, and songs of praise and thanksgiving.

Lord, I know that You watch over my life with perfect love and infinite power. Everything that happens to me, You either will or permit as a means of drawing me closer to You. Sometimes, Lord, when You don't let me have my way I feel anger and resentment swelling inside me. I may even express my feelings as complaints or doubts.

Forgive me, Lord. Help me to see the absurdity of putting my will before Yours. Let me embrace every event in which You deny me something I want. Help me also to look for opportunities to deny myself by giving up legitimate pleasures. Lead me to keep myself fit for Your service in both mind and body.

Supermarket Savings

As we seek to live by God's providence—and according to His economy—what practical measures besides cutting down on the amount we eat can we take to make better use of the money we spend on food?

1. Wise buying is like increasing our income. The money saved by watching for bargains, making out lists and following them, exercising self-discipline, and applying other principles of consumer economics—this money can be put to other uses in serving our fellow human beings.

2. Freezer and other storage space makes it possible to stock up on special purchases. Buying something at a discount, though, doesn't mean we should splurge on things we could well do without. Asking more often, "Do I really *need* this item?" is one of the best devices known to save money.

3. Consider buying the economy size of products you use a lot. This is especially important with non-food items, where savings can often be as high as fifteen or twenty percent.

4. Consider buying store brands, which are often cheaper than those of major food companies. They can

32

save you as much as ten percent on food items and another ten percent on non-edibles, frequently with no difference in quality.

5. Buy lower-grade foods where appearance doesn't matter. Cheaper vegetables used in casseroles or stews, for example, are generally as wholesome and nourishing as those of a higher grade. They just don't look as pretty.

6. You can cut thirty percent or more from your meat bill by buying the less expensive, tougher cuts of meat and marinating them. Pounding the tough cuts with a tenderizing hammer or a regular hammer wrapped in cloth will also help.

7. Take advantage of the normal fluctuations in the prices of meat and eggs to cut your protein bill. Large cuts of meat are often on sale in the summertime, when most people are buying smaller cuts. Stocking your freezer with steak in July will help you avoid the high steak prices of January. Buying lamb in the spring will also save you money. Eggs are cheaper in the winter, when chickens lay more generously.

8. You may be able to save on canned goods by making a deal with your grocer to relieve him of dented cans at a discount. Some areas have stores that specialize in slightly dented cans. Cans that are punctured, bulging, or black around the rim or the dent are dangerous, however.

9. Know the prices of the items you regularly purchase. If a price increases dramatically at one store, check other supermarkets before making the purchase. Sometimes you can find items marked at lower prices that have remained on the shelf for a while.

Lower prices do not always mean lower quality. Overpricing is a common practice. In some industries, as a matter of fact, higher-priced items sell better regardless of quality. Cosmetics manufacturers and advertising agencies know that women feel cheated when they buy beauty products at low prices. Somehow the assumption is that the lower-priced product will not be as effective in making them beautiful.

10. Coupons are an important source of savings at the supermarket. Using them wisely can save you as much as twenty percent of your food cost. Be careful, though, not to buy luxury food or unnecessary quantities of your usual purchases just because you have coupons.

11. Food-buying cooperatives buy food in bulk and offer it to their members. By donating a small amount of your time to help take orders and buy, sort, and distribute groceries to other members, you receive price reductions amounting to a wholesale discount.

12. Do your food shopping after you have eaten. Know what you need, make a list, and stick to it. Every minute over a half-hour that you're in the supermarket will tempt you to buy unnecessary products on impulse.

13. Wednesday and Thursday nights tend to be good times for food shopping. Generally stores are not crowded then, and you're likely to find a plentiful supply of the items you need.

14. Taking children along to the supermarket almost inevitably adds to the amount of money you leave behind at the checkout counter. There are other reasons, of course, why many parents prefer not to have the children along when they shop. Neat stacks of cans present a powerful temptation.

(Despite these drawbacks, I would encourage taking the children along to the supermarket at least periodically. They need to learn what it's like to go shopping. The discipline involved in not being allowed to have every tempting item they see is extremely valuable.)

34

"Meat to Fit Your Pocketbook"

Ten More Quick, General Savings Tips

How we live, then, does make a difference. In our homes, in the marketplace—we as the people of God are to be constantly "on call" to the divine signals of the Holy Spirit, to know and to do the will of the Father. God has called us to be careful stewards of His wealth, and that means being responsible spenders and consumers.

Let me offer a final ten ideas for saving those resources of yours both at home and away:

1. Consolidate your shopping trips to avoid driving to the store repeatedly for separate items. A running grocery list posted in the kitchen will be helpful.
2. Plan your meals around the specials advertised in the newspaper. This works especially well with frozen items.
3. Take advantage of the lower prices on fruits and vegetables as they come into season.
4. Recognize that supermarket managers are smart business people. They'll put the staples you're sure to buy on the bottom shelves and the expensive gourmet treats at eye level.
5. Inexpensive table salt is useful for a variety of household chores. You can use it as a scouring powder for cutting boards, coffee pots, and baking dishes. Mix it with water and pour it down the drain to clear away grease and odor.
6. Ants, roaches, and rats—no matter how clean we are, encounters with these pests are almost inevitable. You can save money by using cheap but effective remedies. Common salt sprinkled across the path of crawling ants will drive them away. Powdered boric acid is an inexpensive roach control. An equal mix of cement powder and kitchen flour will give rats a fatal case of indigestion. (As always, use these remedies only where children cannot get to them.)

7. Toothpaste might serve as a substitute for silver polish. You'll be surprised at the quick shine you can bring to your tarnished utensils.

8. If your locks are sticking, graphite might help. All you need is a pencil: Rub it on the edges of the key before inserting the key into the lock.

9. If the tube of shampoo is nearly empty, try snipping it in half with scissors. You'll probably find enough shampoo for another washing.

10. If you use a lot of paper and don't really need high quality stationery, you can probably find an abundant supply in data processing centers of school districts, universities, or city or county governments. Wastebaskets next to copy machines also yield abundant scrap paper.

4

I Have a Suit for Every Day of the Week— And This Is It

Women's liberation has taken a long time. In the fourteenth century, women were not thought capable of owning anything. The newly married man who wanted to show his confidence in his bride would agree to give her a sum of money every year that she could spend on anything she wanted. Usually this money went for clothing and personal ornaments. Pins to decorate wearing apparel were a new fad at that time, and so the money a woman spent for these accessories came to be known as "pin money."

Diamonds may be a girl's best friend, but mink and sable are good pals also. Clothes are a very important part of our lives. Next to food and shelter, clothing cost is generally the largest family expenditure. Those of us who buy clothes for big families know what it means to be permanently pressed.

It's fairly easy to project future costs of food and shelter for budgeting purposes, but clothing is much more difficult. Clothing costs fluctuate because the types and styles that are fashionable constantly change according to public whim. Also, because clothes must vary with the seasons, budgeting accurately for this category can be tricky.

Obviously the main purpose of clothing is providing protection against bad weather, but there are secondary values that are just as important to consider as we plan expenditures in this area. Clothing is part of the socialization process leading to healthy self-esteem and a sense of identity. Many parents will forego other needs to make sure that children have appropriate clothes. Similarly, adults may sacrifice some planned purchases to invest more money in their physical appearance.

Evaluating Your Wardrobe

Clothing expenditures usually account for ten to fifteen percent of the total family budget. How this money is spent should be a matter of some planning. A good first step is taking inventory of the amount and condition of clothing on hand.

Some of the clothes you have will be suitable to be worn as is; others may be repaired or remodeled. New clothing items that will be needed within the next year or two should be listed in order of urgency. Then an estimate can be made of the amount of money required and available. On this basis priorities can be set.

Much of what you think you need might be hanging in your closet right now. It's in there with those other outfits you wouldn't be caught dead in. (If the shoe fits, it's ugly.) But even from these mistakes, you can learn a great deal.

Take everything out of the closet. Bring out those clothes that have been crammed into the corners and pushed to the back. That includes all those shoes and hats that have been boxed and forgotten. Take time to try everything on, including your favorite suits or dresses. Decide why you wear certain outfits again and again. Do you like them because of the color, the style, the fit, or all of these things?

What you decide you won't wear again, get rid of. Some of these decisions will be difficult, but it's better to let someone else wear something than to keep it hanging idly in your closet. For one thing, a closet crowded with unwearables seems to offer more than it really has. That's confusing and demoralizing. In general, if you haven't worn something for the last couple of years, you probably never will.

Next, try out various combinations. Ladies, put on a jacket over a dress. Men, try combining different shirts and suits. Try out your best sweater with every skirt or pair of trousers you have. Work up complete outfits, including ties, socks, and shoes, for the men, and handbags and accessories for the women. Then make a list of what goes with what and of the specific things you need to make your wardrobe stretch even farther.

Need for Thrift

Most of us could get by on a more limited wardrobe. We fool ourselves into believing that we must have a large variety of clothes in order to maintain an attractive appearance. Actually a few carefully chosen outfits, especially those that offer cross-combinations, are all we really need.

Thrift has been defined as "wanting less than you can afford." In the Christian sense, thrift is making better use of resources—economizing to be able to share with others. Each of us has the responsibility of making the most of what we have. To reinforce this responsibility, Christ gave us the parable of the silver pieces. He described a man who, prior to setting out on a journey, handed his funds over to his servants. He gave one servant five thousand silver pieces, a second two thousand, and a third one thousand. The two who received five thousand and two thousand invested their money and doubled the amount. The servant who received one thousand, on the other hand, buried the money in much the same way as we bury our human endowments.

When the master returned, he commended the servants who had succeeded in doubling their resources. To the servant who had buried his, however, he said, "You worthless, lazy lout! You know I reap where I did not sow and gather where I did not scatter. All the more reason to deposit my money with the bankers so that on my return I could have had it back with interest." He then ordered the unproductive servant to be cast outside into the darkness.

Significantly, Christ noted that the money had been allocated to the servants "according to each man's abilities." The servant who succeeded in doubling his two thousand silver pieces received the same commendation as he who had made five thousand. Unfortunately, many of us who observe that we have fewer gifts than others around us, tend to use those we have poorly. Thus Christ could predict, "Those who have will get more until they grow rich, while those who have not will lose even the little they have" (Matt. 25:29).

Our Throwaway Age

Many women have succeeded in saving a large percentage of their clothing budget by learning to sew. Others make good use of hand-me-downs and second-hand clothing, even though these methods of saving run contrary to a fundamental characteristic of our times. We live in a throwaway age. Almost nothing is made to last. Appliances, toys, and other electrical or mechanical objects seem to be made to self-destruct.

The catch is they don't destroy themselves completely. They just stop working and sit there. Though this can be a problem, it is still easier to purchase new things rather than to have the old ones repaired.

We assume that new products are necessarily better than old, even though we know that the quality of materials and workmanship is usually inferior. Stopping to consider the merits of holding on to what we have takes too much patience and time.

There are at least three questions we should ask ourselves about our throwaway tendencies. These are especially relevant if we have any talent for fixing things:

1. Is there any way I can repair this item instead of throwing it away?
2. Can this item be modified and put to another practical use?

3. Would this item be useful to someone else, either in its present or modified form?

Recycling

A trend toward recycling rather than throwing everything away began just a few years ago. Energy and environmental problems helped spur efforts in this direction. Some examples are the following:

A pilot project at the University of Rhode Island uses a blend of waste lubricating oil and residual industrial oil to help heat the campus. A single year's savings with this project amounted to $28,000.

A school in Minnesota saved an estimated $16,000 in one year by switching from fuel oil to saw mill residues for heating purposes.

With most of the nation's paper mills depending on waste paper for their raw material, about one of every four tons of waste paper is now recycled.

In Colorado, a waste conversion plant converts 350 tons of manure a day into methane gas to generate electricity and into protein for livestock feed.

Consumer Education

All right, then. We can save by buying only what we need, we can save by do-it-yourself techniques, and we can save by using and reusing old things until it is impractical to do so. But this is just the beginning.

Consumer education is an important part of the curriculum of many public schools today. Numerous books have been written to guide the shopper toward wise and economical expenditure. At the risk of oversimplification, much of the content of these courses and books can be reduced to several basic principles. Before approaching these, let me tell you of two methods of saving that probably *won't* work

41

for you. It is said that Marc Chagall, the famous artist, pays for all his purchases—even small items like cigarettes and toothpaste—with personal checks. Chagall found out years ago that most merchants would keep the checks rather than cash them because Chagall's signature makes them valuable collector's items.

Then there was the men's clothing store operator in Concord, California, who had the lowest prices in town. Underselling his rival was legitimate, but his method led to his downfall. What the man did was steal several thousand dollars' worth of merchandise from the rival store and sell it at half price. One day his victim took a detective shopping with him and that was the end of the scheme.

The single most effective way of saving money when you shop is being governed by your reason rather than your emotion. We have a war to win against advertisers who have been trained to extract our dollars from our pockets. We lose thousands through advertising, even though many of us never take out a single ad. The appeal of a new product is increased tremendously by the emotional content of television, magazine, and newspaper advertising.

Avoid impulse buying. If we weigh our purchasing decisions with care, especially when a large sum of money is involved, we're likely to be surprised at how much we can do without while still deriving great enjoyment from what we have.

Shop Around

A second basic principle in saving while shopping is looking for the best prices you can find on items of comparable quality. It does pay to shop around. Rapid inflation has increased the variation in prices of most items, with gasoline as a prime example. Within the area of a few blocks I can usually find gasoline prices that vary as much as ten to even twenty-five percent.

A Suit for Every Day of the Week

In almost any line of purchase, stores charge a range of prices for the same goods and services. One type of price differential, of course, is wholesale versus retail, but actually many prices that appear to be fixed are indeed flexible. We often miss an opportunity to buy at discount because we accept the initially given price as final.

The impression we make on the seller can sometimes make a difference. If I walk into an electrical supply store and let the store manager know how little I know about wiring, he's almost certain to charge me top price or steer me to the most expensive kind. On the other hand, if I read up in advance and identify exactly the kind of wiring I need, I may be able to get the same kind of discount as a craftsman would obtain. At least, I will know the quality I need.

Another technique for buying at reduced prices is to look for small flaws. Every day consumers pay full price for items that should be marked down because of defects. Point up the flaws, make them seem conspicuous enough to discourage other buyers, and shopkeepers may release the item at a substantial discount.

Comparison shopping is crucial, especially for two types of purchase. It is always advisable, of course, to compare prices on relatively expensive items. It might even be productive to use the telephone to contact several merchants before leaving home. At the very least, you'll get an idea of price range and a few of the more promising places to go to look at the item in question.

Saving several hundred dollars on an automobile makes it worth your while to spend time and fuel shopping around for the best deal. In the process you can consider accessories, get a feeling for the kind of service the dealer will provide, and, most important, get the make and model of car that is best for you.

You need a different kind of comparison strategy for products you consume regularly. With these lower-priced items, it is wise to maintain an ongoing kind of price comparison. A chart of regularly purchased food items, for example, would indicate what various supermarkets are charging for these items. Such a chart will show you which store has the most low prices as well as steer you during occasional stock-up visits to a market that has certain items priced lower.

Price comparisons give you a basis for judging what you should pay for a given item. Especially in times of rapid inflation, it's difficult to keep track of what prices are reasonable. How would you know whether paying $49.95 for a certain clock radio is reasonable unless you compare?

Some price comparisons can be done in your own home. Check newspaper and magazine ads or catalogs and maintain a general sense of cost levels, as well as making note of certain specific prices. *Consumer Reports* is another helpful source of information about prices. If you can get this publication from your local library you'll save a few more dollars, the cost of the subscription.

Bargain Stores

In most cities and suburbs thrift shops, often operated by charitable organizations, make it possible to economize on a regular basis. These shops offer an excellent way to furnish a recreation area or a child's room as well as to provide inexpensive clothing for the family.

Recessions cause a depletion in the stock of thrift shops. People tend to keep their own clothes longer and repair other items they would otherwise be giving away. Finding a bargain becomes an even greater challenge. Army-Navy surplus stores have helped many of us by selling shoes, camping supplies, and clothing at considerable savings.

Outlet stores, manufacturer's courtesy stores, factory stores, and discount stores offer goods at low prices with reductions as high as seventy percent. Manufacturer's courtesy stores and factory stores are usually located near the factories where the products are made. First quality products are sold at low prices because there are no shipping charges and overhead is kept to a minimum. These stores also sell irregulars or factory imperfects at even greater savings.

Outlet stores and some discount stores sell overruns or discontinued merchandise, again at substantial savings. And, of course, almost every well-populated area has one or more chain discount stores. Be somewhat cautious if you shop regularly at a discount store; some items will be priced higher than in a regular department store. In general, though, the discount store offers savings on everyday needs and considerable reductions on large purchases such as major appliances.

Price tags in the various types of discount stores usually bear only a single price rather than the original price crossed out with the sale price written in. If you keep up on prices, however, you'll be able to recognize a good buy, especially if the manufacturer's name is familiar to you.

Check the sale item over carefully. There are many reasons why products in these stores are sold at a lower price. If the item is imperfect, be sure to examine the flaw. If you have questions about the product or its price, ask. Finally, if the item fits your need and you are satisfied with its quality, buy it immediately. Comparison shopping among discount stores does not make a great deal of sense. The products turn over rapidly and not everything you want will always be available.

Fairness to the Consumer

The emphasis on the rights of consumers is relatively new in our society. Not too many years ago the consumer had no protection beyond the principle of *caveat emptor*, which translates to "let the buyer beware." The consumer's own alertness and ability to judge the quality of a product were the only safeguards against shoddy merchandise.

Thanks to the efforts of Ralph Nader, David Horowitz, and others, the dignity of the consumer has begun to be considered. For some of us, though, the lesson has yet to hit home. No matter how little we may have to spend, each of us is entitled to the best for our money. As consumers, we are the most important link in the economic chain. Without our contribution the entire economy would collapse.

Part of the responsibility for using resources well is taking a firm enough stand in insisting on fair treatment. Helping to keep merchants honest is a valuable service to our society. No need here for a dissertation on consumer rights, but many of us need some encouragement to speak up when we feel we are treated unfairly.

What recourse does the dissatisfied consumer have? There is the option of returning the merchandise. Most stores honor this privilege, even if there's nothing wrong with what has been purchased. If the consumer decides that he dislikes the color or style of an unaltered suit, he can return it within about a week, provided he hasn't worn it. In some cases, this is true even if the suit has been altered to fit.

What about defective merchandise? Many people assume that unless a written warranty is issued they have no protection against merchandise that is defective. The principle of implied warranty gives the consumer the right to expect the manufacturer to repair or replace a transistor radio that doesn't work or a sweater with a torn seam.

The steps to be followed are simple. Return the merchandise to the store where you bought it. If it should happen that the merchant refuses to take responsibility and refers you to the manufacturer, consider taking future business elsewhere. Get in touch with the manufacturer even if you do not have a warranty. If the difficulty was indeed caused by a defect in the product, you are likely to get a satisfactory response. This depends on the company and on who happens to read your letter. Some manufacturers will replace defective products long after a guarantee has expired, while others refuse to do anything at all. Still, a phone call or letter to the president of the company is usually worth the effort.

Other consumer actions are possible if neither retailer nor manufacturer will give satisfaction. Some newspapers and radio stations operate consumer complaint departments that publicize and follow up claims of unfair treatment. Letters to such departments often bring results. The Better Business Bureau is also worth a try, although in general the Bureau's record of performance in handling consumer complaints is not good. Essentially, the Better Business Bureau is an organization of business people, not of consumers.

There are some government agencies that might be helpful. Most books on consumerism contain listings of such agencies. If you try a federal agency and receive no acknowledgement, a letter to your Congressman will usually get some kind of result.

There are also city and state government agencies to which consumers may bring complaints of mistreatment. In a small town, a letter to the attorney general of the state might be helpful.

Small claims courts exist in a number of cities to handle suits which do not require a lawyer for amounts not exceeding a few hundred dollars. These vary greatly in their effectiveness in handling consumer complaints. Nevertheless, the mere receipt of the summons convinces the firm you are dealing with that you mean business and often produces a settlement.

In conclusion, the individual consumer can do a great deal to help himself. Becoming a smart shopper is the first step. Buyer wariness is still very much in order. No matter how careful you are, though, some things you buy will not meet your expectations. Those are the times to take definite steps of complaint procedure to correct the situation.

Saving Hints

Saving money on your clothing budget is based on three guidelines:

1. Fit the quality to the use.
2. Make the cost of maintenance part of your buying decision.
3. Get a good price.

First, it makes sense to let the quality you look for in a given item of clothing correspond to its use. Choosing the best quality you can afford for the items you wear most is economical. On the other hand, it's foolish to set aside a major portion of your clothing budget to spend on outfits you will wear only rarely.

As we said earlier, try to choose garments and colors that harmonize with one another and are interchangeable. Plan your wardrobe to match and mix sweaters, skirts, jackets, and the like.

Inexpensive but attractive accessories can make a limited wardrobe much more attractive. Many of these you will be able to make yourself. Select the newest colors and extend the variety of your wardrobe by using the accessories in various combinations with your basic outfit.

Small children need comfortable, washable clothing, rather than expensive, high-quality clothes that will last far beyond the time it takes them to outgrow them. With our own children, many of the clothing items we purchased would be well-worn after being passed down only a few times. On the other hand, some of the clothes we obtained from friends made the rounds of all six of our sons and still had some life remaining.

In making decisions about the quality of clothes, don't assume that all expensive items are carefully constructed. Good quality must be paid for, but know enough about clothes to make sure you're getting your money's worth. Here is a suggested quality-check procedure:

A Suit for Every Day of the Week

1. Turn the garment inside out. Check the seams. Make sure they are overstitched or pinked so that they won't ravel. At the end of the seam, check that the stitches are retraced to insure that the threads aren't left hanging. Seams should be wide enough to resist pulling at stress points.
2. Check all knits to make sure that there are no holes or snags.
3. Material bunching around a zipper or a placket is a sign of poor construction.
4. Side seams and underarm seams should meet. Shoulder seams should meet any side seams on the collar.
5. Stripes or patterns should be matched exactly at the seams.
6. Check the hang of the material. Some fabrics lose their shape and wrinkle easily. If the garment doesn't look good on a hanger, it probably won't look good on you. Furs, buttons, and snaps should not pull. When you try on the garment, make sure the zippers, buttons, and snaps close without straining the material.

Sometimes we make the mistake of choosing an item on the basis of purchase price without considering future maintenance costs. A washable garment might cost more than one that has to be dry cleaned, but in the long run it will probably be a better bargain. This is especially true of clothing that is light in color and will quickly show soil. Wash-and-wear and permanent press items provide convenience as well as economy. Spot-repellant fabrics, surface-treated to resist stains, will not allow spills to penetrate the weave, thus reducing their maintenance costs.

Taking good care of clothes helps to keep them in use for a longer time. The manufacturer's recommendations about special methods of washing or cleaning always should be followed. Try to take care of stains and repairs without delay. Never store a garment that has not been cleaned and be sure to provide adequate protection against moths.

(You might reserve one end of your closet for garments that need washing, cleaning, or repair. Keep the things you wear often in a readily accessible position and figure out a flexible rotation plan for these outfits.)

Learn about the fibers and fabrics from which clothing is made. Investigate synthetic materials and the manufacturer's trade names for them. Knowing the durability, convenience, and care requirements of acetate, acrylic, and polyester may help you to make wiser purchasing decisions.

Knowing the quality most appropriate for the clothing items you are buying and with an eye toward future maintenance costs, you can now set about getting the best price you can. Shop around. Discount stores and bargain basements offer many opportunities for savings, as do clearance sales at specialty shops and independent clothing stores. Planning your purchases ahead of time will help you take advantage of sales, especially if you can get to the store early enough to have a wide selection.

The advertising announcing a sale will often indicate if it is an opportunity to be pursued. Sales that are advertised at "fifty percent off " are usually poor risks. The "limited time only" that goes on and on should also arouse your suspicion. On the other hand, regular merchandise reduced for clearance will often carry prices well below those normally charged.

5

When We Asked to See a House in Our Price Range, the Realtor Showed Us One With a Moon in the Door

It takes a heap o' money to make a house your own, so some words of warning—and encouragement—are in order. In this chapter, we will discuss building, buying, and renting homes.

Because a home represents such a large investment, it pays to be careful. A Knoxville, Tennessee, man wanted to build himself a home. He obtained the services of a good architect, and the building got under way. Everything seemed to proceed very smoothly, and in due time the man was delighted with the new house he owned. Just as he was ready to move in, though, the city authorities brought him some bad news. He owned the house, but not the ground under it. His property title was for lot 17, and he had built his home on lot 175!

In building, buying, or renting our dwellings, as in all other phases of living, we would do well to heed Christ's advice: "If one of you decides to build a tower, will he not first sit down and calculate the outlay to see if he has enough money to complete the project? He will do that for fear of laying the foundation and then not being able to complete the work . . ." (Luke 14:28,29).

What the Master Craftsman says about building a high-rise applies as well to a modest home in suburbia. Count the cost before you start. Our Lord wasn't finished, though; He concluded with an even more important point: "In the same way, none of you can be my disciple if he does not renounce

51

all his possessions" (Luke 14:33). Like building a tower, following Christ entails a cost, and we should be prepared to pay that cost (note: "*all* his possessions") before we start the project.

Remember, then, you must give the home you are building or buying over to the Lord. What does this mean? Well, for one thing, it means you'll try to get the kind of home you think Christ might have if He were in your shoes. It means you will try to economize on nonessentials to have more money for serving others.

The Cost of a Home

Your investment in a dwelling represents one of the single greatest opportunities you have for economizing. If, like most of us, you decide to buy a home on the outskirts of your income, you'll be paying for it for a long time. I've heard it said that if you've always aspired to write something that will live forever, all you have to do is sign a mortgage.

Whether you are building or buying someone else's house, have a good idea of what you can afford. Although common sense is your best guide, there are two formulas helpful in avoiding poor judgment. Consider these as rules of thumb, rather than precise determinations.

The first guideline is to limit the cost of your home to twice your annual income. If the annual family income totals $30,000 you probably ought to look for a home in the $60,000 price range.

Second, estimate the monthly cost for mortgage payments, taxes, insurance, and utilities, and compare this with the family income for a week. Since these items should comprise about twenty-five percent of your budget, you'll be on fairly safe ground if a week's pay covers such expenses for a month. Inflation has made it difficult to stay within this guideline, but if you must put more into housing, you'll have to cut food and clothing costs or other expenses.

A House in Our Price Range

There are many other factors to be considered, of course, which is why common sense is crucial. The possibility of dramatic decreases or increases in family income should be considered. You also need to anticipate any unusual expenses that will detract from your ability to meet the mortgage payments.

If you are conservative, you might consider the possibility that you can afford more house than you think you can. What funds are put into your home will form a saving base that will hold up against future inflation.

There's no doubt that buying an expensive home means housing costs will consume a large percentage of your income. Especially in the early stages of ownership, restraint, sacrifice, and meticulous budgeting will be necessary before, in time, the imbalance corrects itself. As the years go by, your income will probably increase, and the payments will be less difficult. Meanwhile, you will have earned equity in your home through the payments you have made on the principal and the appreciation of the property.

One of the most serious mistakes home buyers make is trying to force themselves into a life-style that is unnatural for them. Sometimes this is simply a matter of buying a home in a neighborhood where they will not be comfortable. Even if they are successful in meeting the mortgage payments, they find themselves ill at ease with neighbors, the schools, or available services in the community.

A more common problem is trying to straightjacket oneself with a budget that is too tight. Investing in a home should cause some cuts in your spending, but the plans you make for cutting must be reasonable; you will still need some recreation, an occasional new outfit, and at least a small contingency fund.

Home buying entails many other expenses besides the building itself. When you move to the suburbs, for example, one thing you discover is that trees grow on money. One suburbanite commented, "I took up gardening and developed a green thumb. I got it from pulling twenties from my wallet at the nursery." And if the realtor tells you a house is maintenance-free, what he means is that there hasn't been any maintenance for a long time.

Your Mortgage

Another decision to be made when buying a home is the type of mortgage. There are usually several types available, the most common of which will be described below.

The *graduated payment* mortgage provides a lower initial monthly payment than a standard mortgage. The intent is to have the payments increase in pace with your income. After a while, the payment is fixed at a somewhat higher level than the standard mortgage, so that the loan can be repaid within the specified time period.

A *variable rate* mortgage includes a provision for changing the interest rate according to the cost of living. Interest on loans moves up and down within strict limits, allowing the lender to raise interest rates on outstanding loans when the cost of money increases. Similarly, when the cost of funds drops, interest rates and payments decline.

The *portable* mortgage is actually a variable rate type. Here the borrower can take his or her present mortgage along in the purchase of a new home without incurring higher interest rates than those justified by the current cost of money.

Another variation is the *rollover* mortgage. Under this plan, the mortgage loan is made for a specified short-term period, usually three to five years. When this term ends, the mortgage is renegotiated at a new rate of interest. The typical rollover mortgage has a five percent restriction on increasing interest rates.

For low income families, there are special federal provisions to reduce interest and subsidize the lender. Monthly government assistance is paid to the lender to bring the home owner's interest rate down to as little as four percent. Families are required to pay twenty percent of their adjusted income under this type of provision.

Obtaining a Home Loan

When you look for a mortgage on your home, it pays to shop around. Check all possible sources of loans to get the most reasonable interest rate. Most often a savings and loan association will offer lower rates than a commercial bank, but there are exceptions. A bank that has some surplus funds not immediately designated for business loans may be able to offer you lower interest. You might get a better deal from an insurance company or a mortgage company.

Obviously, the more you are able to put into a down payment, the shorter will be the period of your mortgage or the lower your monthly charges. Most of us, when we are buying our first home, need the smallest possible down payment, which is generally twenty percent on the conventional mortgage. Veterans Administration loans, however, make it possible to obtain a mortgage with no down payment. Federal Housing Administration loans require only a modest amount to be put down.

Be sure that the terms of your mortgage loan provide for prepayment without penalty. The sooner you pay off the loan, the less your total cost will be. On the other hand, you don't want the term of the loan to be so short that your monthly payments are more than you can afford. Thirty-year loans have become common for this reason. If you take a thirty-year mortgage and your financial resources improve considerably, you might want to pay off the mortgage sooner. In this case you'll want to make sure that your savings in interest are not lessened by a prepayment penalty.

A primary consideration in the decision whether to pay off a loan ahead of time is prevailing interest rates. If the interest rate you obtained on your loan is lower than current interest rates, it makes good sense not to pay off the loan even though your financial condition improves dramatically. You'll be able to invest the money at a higher rate than you are paying on your mortgage loan.

Home-Buying Savings

Is it better to invest in a fancy house in a run-down neighborhood or a shack in a more exclusive location? Go for a good location. If you buy an attractive home in a poor neighborhood, you're facing future decline in property values. A home you can improve in a better section of town will bring you increased value over the years.

If you are buying a home in a new housing development, the frills, such as shutters, planters, and corner cabinets, will be costly if the developer supplies them. The same holds true for washer, dryer, refrigerator, and stove. Contract with the developer for the basic house before he builds it and add these extras yourself. The only exception to this is if you buy the model house in a subdivision, which the developer is often willing to sell for little profit.

If you're planning to build your own home or have it built, you may be able to get a bargain on the lot. Check the county records for land held for nonpayment of taxes. If you find something attractive, have the land appraised and negotiate with the county appraiser for a fair price. Some counties hold annual public auctions to sell tax-delinquent land. As the successful bidder on such a piece of property, you'll probably have to wait two years to give the previous owner an opportunity to pay back taxes. There is no risk, though, because even if the original owner reclaims the land, your investment will be returned with interest.

The plan you select for your home can also be a source of savings. A rectangular floor plan, rather than a U- or L-shaped one, will decrease the cost per square foot. A two-story house will cut roof costs in half, while a plan that includes a basement can double your living space for a fraction of the normal space cost. A kitchen and bathroom back to back can use the same water lines.

Your Money's Worth

Of the hundreds of questions you might ask when you inspect a home, some are more important than others. Let me list just ten questions that are crucial in helping you get your money's worth:

1. How does the asking price compare with a real-estate appraiser's estimate of the fair market value of the home?
2. What does a construction expert have to say about the quality of the construction and the need for repairs and improvements?
3. Considering the value of the home and the character of the neighborhood, are you likely to be able to sell the home for more than you are paying for it?
4. What are the total annual real-estate taxes on this property?
5. What can previous buyers tell you about their satisfaction with this builder's homes?
6. What kind of warranty comes with the house?
7. Is the location of the house suited to your needs?
8. Is the floor plan of the house suited to your needs?
9. Does the heating system have a reasonable guarantee?
10. Is the house well located on its lot to provide privacy, good exposure, and favorable relation to the sun?

Building Your Own Home

If you are building, giving your home over to Christ should mean that you ask the Lord's help in finding a reputable, cooperative contractor who will deal with you honestly. You have no alternatives but to trust your builder a great deal, and you will want assurance that he deserves your trust.

Some years ago, very close friends of ours had their dream house built. It was a new home in a very attractive residential neighborhood. Fifteen years they had saved to provide themselves and their family with a wonderful place to live. Unfortunately, the builder they hired was unethical. After being paid his fee, he did not pay the subcontractors and later declared bankruptcy. Our friends were left with numerous bills from these subcontractors and were forced to give up their dream home and move into more modest quarters.

Ask any builder you are considering to give you the names of the owners of the five most recent homes he has built. Contact these people to see how satisfied they are. Carefully inspect the blueprints and the building contract. Your contract can't include every important point; that's where trust comes in. But it should contain sufficiently detailed provisions to clarify the builder's responsibility to deliver a specific home within a specific time period.

No matter how careful your selection of builder and your preliminary planning, you won't be one hundred percent satisfied with your new home. A few nightmares occur in the building of every dream house, no matter how perfect your planning. Like every other human product, your home will have some imperfections.

Let's talk about a few of the most common problems encountered in a newly constructed home. Popped nails are common. The lumber in the frame of any home is bound to change in size and shape with changes in temperature and humidity. The nails in the wood and the wallboard over it do not bend and thus, as the lumber moves, the nails pop out. You can expect your builder to repair the popped nails. Most builders, however, will not repaint the walls damaged by the nails, though they should leave touch-up paint behind so that you can cover the spots yourself.

Other defects sometimes occur in the drywall. Any readily visible defect, beyond a hairline crack that can be hidden by normal repainting, should certainly be the responsibility of the builder. Walls free from dents and glaring gaps between the wallboard panels are your right.

You can also insist your home be free of drafts around the windows and doors. Under certain temperature and wind conditions, you'll have a small amount of air passage. It is the builder's responsibility, though, to check out these areas to insure that air leakage is within reasonable limits. Proper weather stripping and insulating should correct the problem.

Other kinds of problems can show up in new homes: uneven floors, water leakage, unfinished work, etc. Sometimes it's difficult to establish whose responsibility it should be to repair the problem. Not everything is the builder's fault. If your movers, for example, crash into a door frame with a piece of furniture, the builder is not responsible for repairing the damage. On the other hand, if a bathroom fixture is chipped, your builder should repair or replace the fixture. In general, most reputable builders are willing to incur extra expense in order to ensure customer satisfaction.

Renting

Not every person responsible for keeping a roof overhead can or should own a home. The decision whether to buy or rent is a very important one. In making this decision personal preferences play a predominant role. It s impossible to set down rules of thumb to guide the decision, but there are several main factors one should consider.

The first of these is flexibility. Flexibility is the ability to make quick and easy changes to suit changing needs. Generally speaking, renting offers more flexibility than buying. If you lease a home, you make a commitment that will decrease that flexibility somewhat. Still, leasing offers more flexibility than buying. If substantial changes in your situation seem likely within the next three to five years, leasing will probably make it possible to adapt to those changes more easily. On the other hand, if your future looks fairly stable for at least five years or more, it might make more sense for you to look for a home to purchase.

A second major factor to consider is economy. On the surface it would look more economical to invest your money in a home where you would have something to show for it. Generally this is true, but unless you strike it rich, you will have to pay interest on the mortgage loan. Property taxes and maintenance costs add up—probably beyond your anticipation. These simple financial factors must be considered.

There are several other advantages to renting a house. Draining your capital resources for a down payment on a home is no longer necessary. You are free of the long-term debt that goes with a home mortgage. Worries evaporate about real estate tax increases or home maintenance.

Prestige may be important to some in deciding whether to rent or to buy. Sometimes families strive for living quarters that are chosen more to impress others than to meet their own needs. This can lead us to deep trouble. We may get ourselves hopelessly in debt by purchasing a home beyond our means, when all we can handle is monthly rent. On the other hand, it is also easy to sign a lease for a rental amount that chews up too much of our budget.

Finally we come down to the question of personal needs and desires. Some of us are much more comfortable as apartment dwellers than we could ever be in our own home. We would miss the activity and closeness that often come with apartment living. On the other hand, many families need the privacy of owning a home and could never adjust to apartment living. Each of us has our own needs, goals, and desires. A discussion among family members can create the communication that should be the basis of the decision whether to buy or to rent.

A House in Our Price Range

Finding Your Apartment

As every landlord knows, satisfied tenants are a rare breed. Someone once defined rent as the money you pay the landlord for the privilege of complaining.

In Brooklyn, New York, a tenant complained to the landlord that strange and loud noises were coming from the next apartment. He said it sounded like a herd of elephants. The landlady investigated. Unknown to her the tenant had moved out and left a scruffy little pony behind. He had written her a note: "This place is built like a barn."

For twenty-five years, the occupants of a building in Pittsburgh, Pennsylvania, complained about the trouble they had adjusting the temperature of the building. The higher the thermostat, they claimed, the colder the temperature. When warm weather came, turning down the thermostat seemed to make the building hotter.

That's really the way it was, of course. The whole building had been supplied with thermostats in good working order, but with covers marked in reverse. When occupants tried to cool the building, they were actually turning on the heat.

Even though you may never be completely satisfied, care in selecting your apartment will be well rewarded. If you're a stranger in town, a rental agency may be a good starting place. Much time and effort can sometimes be saved by consulting someone familiar with neighborhoods and the lodging they provide. You should be aware, though, that agencies get most of their listings from newspaper ads, and their fees can be substantial.

If you're not in a hurry to find your living quarters, it is worth your while to explore possible neighborhoods. Look for vacancy signs, take time to meet building superintendents, and talk with residents and shopkeepers.

Once you're serious about a neighborhood, spend some evening hours there. List the qualities important to you, the benefits you really want in your apartment and neighborhood. Check such features as the security of the building; availability of police, fire, and medical services; neatness, safety, and comfort features; convenience of stores and recreational facilities.

Check your lease very carefully before signing it. One big problem in our world is that it's easier to break a commandment than a lease. Each blank should be filled in correctly. The amount of rent should be accurately stated and all promises made by the landlord or rental agent spelled out in the lease agreement. Even if the lease seems perfectly in order, it might be a good idea to have it checked over by your lawyer or someone else familiar with real estate law.

Depending on where you live, certain rental provisions inserted in lease agreements may be illegal. If you find such provisions in your contract, do not sign it. Report it to the authorities.

Examples of such illegal clauses are:

1. A stipulation that the landlord may take your personal property if you don't pay the rent.
2. A clause forcing you to continue to pay rent if the dwelling has been severely damaged by a disaster.
3. A clause forcing you to accept the blame in any dispute with the landlord.
4. A provision that the landlord may retaliate with eviction or other action if you report housing code violations or make other complaints.

Where to Complain

In every rental or lease agreement, there is a large gray area between the specified responsibilities of landlord and tenant. A reputable landlord will do everything he reasonably can to keep a building in satisfactory condition. Nevertheless, a landlord who seems very easy to get along with when you sign the agreement might subsequently resist your efforts to get reasonable complaints settled.

Perhaps you have a serious plumbing problem, and you call your landlord or building manager. Days, weeks, or months might go by—if you let them—without any action being taken. Obviously, it's important that you follow through with proven complaint procedures to get this problem, or any similar injustice, righted.

Let's suppose that you have written your complaint letter and waited an appropriate amount of time for a response. You've heard nothing. What then? If your problem involves other tenants, too, consider banding together in seeking a satisfactory resolution. When the problem is yours alone, you have four basic alternatives:

You might decide that it isn't worth a struggle. You can make the repairs yourself and pay the cost out of your own pocket. This may save considerable time, energy, and frustration.

Usually, though, that's just taking the easy way out. A second possibility is making the repairs yourself and deducting an appropriate amount from the next month's rent. Local law varies considerably on this point, and you'll need to know where you stand legally since your landlord is sure to challenge your decision.

A third possibility is simply withholding rent until the repairs are made. Again, there's danger in this. Your local tenant organization or lawyer should be able to tell you how likely it is that you'll be evicted and how the court might look upon the legitimacy of your complaint.

Your fourth alternative is appealing to local authorities who might pressure the landlord until the problem is corrected. Such authorities include city agencies like the health department, fire department, human rights commission, consumer affairs department, or building inspection department. Also, the secretary of state, division of licenses, and the attorney general at the state level might be helpful. A number of outside agencies, such as a tenant council or the Better Business Bureau, are also worth considering.

Moving

An estimated 40 million Americans move every year. Our transient society seems to know little of the traditional reverence for a home. In the old days, that "heap o' livin'" that went into making a house a home added substantially to the value of the residence. Of course you could never recover this investment; it simply did not translate into dollars. That's one more reason why so many people used to stay put.

One sure way to make your home look better in your eyes is to go out and price some new ones. We have lived in our home for over twenty-five years. Even though we always wanted a large family, we built it as a three-bedroom home because that's all we could afford at the time. We have often talked of moving, but each time we have followed our hearts and expanded and accommodated. We closed in a breezeway and made a bedroom of it. We finished the basement and put another bedroom there. I'm very glad we did. Each time I come home, I am welcomed by familiar things. The warmth of fond memories gives me a security that simply cannot be bought.

But what's right for the Felixes might not be right for you. We have friends who have gained financial profit and enjoyment from buying homes, living in them long enough to remodel them, and then moving on. That's their style; you know yours.

If you do move, for whatever reason, you may find it a difficult experience. Let's conclude this chapter with a few suggestions that might take some of the pain out of moving:

1. Use a professional, licensed moving company. Almost certainly you'll be able to find someone who will promise to do the job more cheaply than a licensed mover can. But unless this more reasonable offer comes from a very trusted friend with the muscles and equipment necessary to do a good job, you are almost certain to pay more in the long run.

2. Ask for references and talk to people who have hired the company in the past. Request and examine a copy of the company's performance record. If the company is engaged in interstate moving, they must provide such a report to you upon request.

3. Obtain an estimate of how much it will cost you to move. The mover should come to your home and size up the task. Even though a precise figure is impossible until your furnishings have been weighed, it will be more accurate than just a telephone guess.

4. Check to see whether the moving company will honor credit cards at the end of the move. This will give you added leverage in resolving complaints.

5. Make an exact inventory of everything you ship. List visible defects or scratches on your belongings before they are moved. Examine the contract and the bill of lading with care.

6. Have your inventory list handy at the time of departure. The movers will prepare their own inventory and want you to sign it. Don't sign before comparing the two inventories and making a notation on the master list of any variations.

6

When I Open the Mail, I Feel Bilious

The other day I received three items in the mail. The first was an ad from my friendly neighborhood Cadillac dealer. The second was just another piece of junk mail. "For centuries," the brochure announced, "gold has been the currency accepted everywhere." I turned to the third item, a statement from my bank. It read, "Balance from previous statement, .00; amounts of checks and debits, .00; amounts of deposits and credits, .00; statement balance, .00." Then, as if to drive the needle a bit deeper, the computer had printed on the statement, "Looking for a smart way to invest your money?"

Some years ago, in Miami Springs, Florida, a crowd of residents rushed to pay overdue water bills. The surprised clerk said, "I never saw anything like it. They came dashing in as fast as they could with the money in their hands." Later, the reason for the hurry became apparent. A road grading machine had accidentally cut a main water line, shutting off the supply. Unaware of what had taken place, the residents assumed that their water had been turned off for failure to pay their bills.

When the end of the month finds you wondering how you will get all your bills paid, consider the birds of the air. They have bills, too, but they just keep on singing. In this chapter I'd like to suggest some ways that might help you do the same. We'll talk about saving on energy and utility costs and about the wise use of credit. When you add these ideas to the information in the last three chapters about clothing, food, and shelter, you'll be ready to make some worthwhile changes in how you are using your financial resources.

Conserving Energy

Many words have been written and spoken in the last few years about the critical shortage of fuel. For most of us, though, the prospect of running out of fuel isn't as seriously threatening as having to pay the bill each month. The simple truth of the matter seems to be that inexpensive fuel is entirely a thing of the past.

The two hundred years from the early 1600s to the early 1800s in our country were a time of abundant, cheap wood fuel. We cut trees with abandon, which amazed Europeans used to the scarcity of wood. Here it was virtually free, to be used without any thought of conservation. Gradually, we depleted our forest resources, and a problem seemed to be forming. Then came coal—a cheap fuel for a century of rapid industrialization.

There followed an even cheaper source of energy, oil, and with it the related product, natural gas. Despite rapid consumption, fuel costs were low because of what seemed to be a rich abundance of supply. Around 1965, though, we used up our surplus, and oil imports increased dramatically. Our era of low fuel costs came to an end. In 1973 we encountered gasoline shortages that seriously affected our lives, which were then made worse by the rise in the cost of fuel oil by rapid spurts.

Now we're wondering whether there will be any end to the price increases. We're told that gasoline was one of the few products for which the price declined, in real terms, in the period up to 1973. Present prices are merely restoring parity with other products—a rationale that doesn't make us any more thankful for the cost of a tankful.

Most of us feel the impact of these increases primarily

through our automobiles. We'll save our discussion of how to get more out of the gold in your gas tank until a later chapter. For now, let's consider a few of the ways you can economize on energy costs at home.

First, the obvious bears repeating. If your attic has no insulation or heat, you can save hundreds of dollars every year by having it insulated. Some homes have a few inches of fiberglass insulation; it's possible to save by adding more. Many older homes have no insulation at all in the outside walls, adding appreciably to heating costs. If you're not sure whether you have such insulation, check the openings around your electrical outlet boxes on these walls. Insulation can be blown or pumped in, and it will more than pay for itself in energy savings.

There are other things you can do to save energy. Regular windows waste a great deal of heat while storm windows can cut heat loss by as much as fifty percent. Also, you can keep the temperature turned low—a principal thrust of the federal program to conserve energy. This is especially effective at night since research has shown that decreasing the heat by eight degrees at night can save ten percent or more on annual fuel costs.

In your attempt to economize, it would also be helpful for you to know which of your appliances use the most electricity. A recent study shows that, with normal usage, the top ten are as follows:

water heater	350 kwhr/month
room airconditioner	321 kwhr/month
refrigerator/freezer	152 kwhr/month
freezer	147 kwhr/month
refrigerator	101 kwhr/month
range	109 kwhr/month
clothes dryer	83 kwhr/month
color television	55 kwhr/month
dehumidifier	31 kwhr/month
dishwasher	30 kwhr/month

Electricity and Water

Cutting back on the use of some of these appliances will certainly ease your monthly utility bills. Here are some specific ideas for cutting the cost of electricity and water:

1. Wash dishes by hand some of the time. Cutting dishwasher usage in half saves about $30 a year on your utility bills. Even though the dishwasher uses less water, it's all hot, and the water heater is probably your most expensive appliance to operate.
2. Skip the drying cycle of the dishwasher. Open the door and let the dishes dry quickly or let them sit in the dishwasher over night.
3. When washing clothes, use a cold water rinse. For six loads of wash a week, you'll save about seven cents a load, or almost $25 a year.
4. Hanging clothes to dry rather than using an electric dryer saves another $25 a year. If you must use the dryer, collect full loads, and be sure the lint filter is clean to obtain maximum efficiency.
5. Take showers instead of baths; they use only about half as much water.
6. Use fluorescent fixtures wherever possible. They provide four times as much light for your money.
7. Repair leaky water faucets as soon as they start dripping. The same slow dripping that was used in Oriental torture can contribute a lot to your budgetary anxieties.

Even with these efforts, though, we're not likely to be as successful as the group of Benedictine nuns in Erie, Pennsylvania, who found a very unusual way to save energy dollars. With heating and electric bills soaring and cutting rapidly into their savings, the sisters took their last $10,000 from the bank and hired a crew to drill a wildcat natural gas well. Then they prayed very hard. At 2,700 feet, the drilling crew hit a gusher. The sisters figure their new supply of natural gas could save them as much as $50,000 over a twenty-five-year period.

How Little We Know

One could say we're paying dearly for the comfort and convenience of modern technology. Few of us, however, would trade our present living styles, expensive as they are, for those our grandparents knew. When we consider the great advances that modern science has realized, we marvel. The human mind has shown itself to be wonderfully powerful indeed!

The truth is, we've just begun. We can never know what things we don't know. We can never appreciate what we have yet to discover. Occasionally we are reminded of the real limitation of our knowledge. A belief we have clung to for a long time becomes a myth exploded. We uncover a mind-boggling truth in an area in which we thought we had comprehensive knowledge. Or, we are brought face to face with the imperfection of our advanced technology.

A gentleman in Evesham, England, saved up cigarette coupons to get a watch. It took a long time; he needed 2000 coupons. Finally he had enough accumulated and sent them off to the tobacco company. Patiently, he waited for his watch to come. As the weeks went by, he began to realize something was wrong. He wrote to the company for an explanation.

Shortly thereafter, three watches arrived in the mail. Since he had ordered only one, he returned two of them. This the computer was totally unable to handle. It went wild. In rapid succession, the man received ten packages one day, nineteen the next, and ten more the day after that—all from the tobacco company. The gifts included three tape recorders, a golf bag, a cot, two electric blankets, a doll, saucepans, a pressure cooker, and record albums.

The man, honest gentleman that he was, sat down and

wrote the tobacco company a letter asking them to look into the matter. Identifying the computer error, the company gave him 10,000 coupons in compensation for his trouble. With these he ordered a bedspread and some tools. The computer sent him two stepladders and a plant stand.

Similar reminders of our limitations are all around us. Consider, for example, the electric light bulb. In 1933 the typical light bulb was rated for 1,000 hours of usage. With our modern advances, most household bulbs today are rated for only 750 hours of use. Around the turn of the century, the Shelby Electric Company was producing light bulbs. Apparently the bulbs the company produced were so good that people didn't buy enough of them. In 1901 a Shelby light bulb was installed in the Livermore, California, fire department. Seventy-five years later it was still burning.

Around our house, we're lucky to get seventy-five days from any one of innumerable bulbs, most of which seem to be on most of the time. Sometimes I feel we need a part-time handyman just to repair electrical fixtures and replace bulbs. Of course, the electric bill is so high we could never afford his salary.

The Cost of Light

Besides keeping us aware of our own limitations, burned-out light bulbs provide another kind of reminder. We're reminded that any time there is light, something is being consumed. Let me switch from earthly to heavenly energy for a moment.

Christ has chosen us to be "the light of the world." If we are to embrace our calling, we must be ready for what light costs. It's going to take something out of us. On the other hand, if we aren't consumed by giving light, we'll be consumed by rotting or rusting. We might as well do our best to let our light shine before men.

Not long ago I was walking through a lamp store, searching for a new kitchen light fixture. All around me were beautiful lamps—so many crowded into so small a space that I could scarcely turn around without fear of knocking one to the floor. Many of the lamps were plugged into an electrical conduit. These gave off the light that enhanced not only their own beauty but also the attractiveness of the lamps that surrounded them.

We need to be plugged in to the conduit of God's love. Christ has given us a model of dynamic divine energy. The word *energy* comes from the Greek and means "working within." The power of God working within us lights up our lives. From time to time, though, our God-given energy seems to go dead or to be short-circuited. Whatever inspiration for living we may have had in the past dries up.

We usually feel most burned out after some severe emotional strain. Perhaps it's the loss of a loved one. Or even some crisis in our lives that has a happy outcome. We invest so much of our inner resources in going through this kind of experience that when it's over we feel completely spent.

The same feeling can exist without being traceable to a specific event. We wake up one morning, and our zest for living is suddenly gone. Just reaching out to grab a toothbrush or a pair of pants seems to take more energy than we can muster. The middle or the end of a day are other possible times for a drop in energy level. Some important task in our lives may not be completed as long as we stay in this state.

What can we do at a time like this? Do we simply turn the entire matter over to God in a spirit of resignation and wait for His energy to "come alive" again? Or is there a way we can reach out and tap God's powerful energy at will?

The truth seems closer to the first possibility. God's energy is not something we can turn on of our own power or make use of as we will. We can only seek to clear the way as best we can for the Spirit to work within us. We can try to root out the selfish tendencies that detract from the efficiency of our service. Mostly we need simply to realize that God's power is always there, even when we are unable to feel its influence.

Hold the Phone

History has known many tyrants and troublemakers. Have you ever felt that the name of Alexander Graham Bell should be somewhere near the top of the list? It seems to me that most of the traumas of my life have been somehow related to the telephone. The boss won't let me make personal calls at work and my wife and kids won't let me make them at home. Whenever I step outside and lock the door behind me, I can count on the telephone ringing. I understand that the bathtub was invented about 3000 B.C. and the telephone in 1876. Imagine all that time to soak without being interrupted by the phone.

Seriously, I do have some unusual hangups about the telephone (now there's a really bad pun!). My understanding of these reactions—their causes and impact on my life—is limited. It is obvious to me, though, that God wants me to do my best to wrestle with these difficulties. A mature adult should not have to struggle long with himself to pick up the phone and call a stranger when there is nothing very threatening about the nature of the call. Calls from people I know should not bring me the feeling that others are intruding on my world.

I'm much too eager to retreat into the safe motel room of my heart and turn the knob that swings up the "Do Not Disturb" signal. My introverted personality feeds an often unhealthy need to be safe from interruption. Important as this defense mechanism might be for my psychological survival, too often I inadvertently cut off a great deal of excitement and fulfillment.

My perspective should be that the ringing of the telephone brings God's will to me. The caller may want some advice, may have an important message to deliver, or may simply be seeking to fulfill a basic need for human communication. In any event, I need to work at receiving such calls openly and willingly. In this perspective, there's something compelling about the ringing of the telephone bell. Mystery lurks there, a determined curiosity to find out who's calling, what God has next in store.

Being open to interruptions won't solve all the frustrations, of course. We'll still get our fair share of wrong numbers. Not long ago in San Diego, the Pacific Telephone Company launched a county-wide project to improve phone service. As part of the project, they changed the telephone numbers of hundreds of residents in San Diego's Pacific beach area. Unfortunately, they didn't tell the customers.

"We were supposed to mail out the final notices telling people their new numbers and about the change," a spokesman explained. The company's postage machine broke down, though, and the letters couldn't be mailed.

Another telephone-related frustration is not being able to find a pencil to jot down a message. We always have plenty of pencils around the house. Whenever our supply runs low, I begin to look for a sale and then buy up a bunch. We also have a pencil sharpener—in good working condition. It remains something of a mystery to me, therefore, that whenever I'm on the telephone and need to record a message, the only pencil available is a stub that hasn't had a point since we used it on our 1970 taxes.

Somewhere I read that about a billion and a half lead pencils are used every year in our country. This amounts to about nine for each man, woman, and child in the United States. Well, each of the eight kids in our family, I would guess, uses up or loses about 400 a year. That totals 3,200 and clears the way for about 344 other people to get along entirely on ball point pens.

Trimming Telephone Bills

There is no question that the telephone has become a crucial communication device in our world. I acknowledge its value—probably one of the greatest bargains we can get for our money. I promise to try to be more appreciative.

Meanwhile, here is a list of suggestions for trimming your telephone bills:

1. Postage is cheaper. It pays to take a few moments to ask whether it's really important to make a long-distance call. Oral communication has much to recommend it, but sometimes a letter will do the job even better. A businessperson has to pay a secretary to transcribe and type correspondence. At home you get to do your own and save money in the process.

2. Think about your toll calls. If many of your friends and relatives live outside your local calling area, you might consider a plan available in various parts of the country called "optional calling" or some similar name. For a monthly fee you are allowed unlimited calls to other geographical areas for a lower price than the regular long-distance rate.

3. Whenever possible, dial your own calls. Any time an operator helps you with a call, you'll pay more than if you had completed the same call yourself. This applies to person-to-person calls, collect calls, credit card charges, and billing to a number other than the one from which you are dialing.

4. Make your long-distance calls at bargain time periods. Long-distance rates are based on airline mileages and on the time at the calling point. You can save a considerable amount by making most of your long-distance calls after 11 at night or on Saturday or Sunday.

5. Limit the length of your long-distance calls. Get yourself a timer if you call long-distance frequently. Before you make a call, organize your thoughts so that you can say what is necessary as briefly as possible.

6. Cut down on expensive rental equipment. Fancy telephones, extensions, and other optional equipment can appreciably increase your telephone bill. Be aware of

how much you are paying for this equipment and for other special services such as Call Forwarding. Be sure that the benefits you derive from the services and equipment justify the expenditure.

7. If you are ordering new phone service, it's a good idea to have jacks installed in every room. It won't cost you much more at the time, and it will save installation charges later if you want to add extensions.

8. Check your phone bills every month. Make sure you are not being charged for wrong numbers and cutoffs. If you are ever billed for an unfamiliar call, don't hesitate to ask for an explanation.

Paying Our Debts

Still another unpleasant item the postman brings us is the monthly statement of our accounts with creditors. Your first statement from the finance company will show you what they really mean by prurient interest. And if you don't understand why they call them personal loans, just miss a payment and see how personal they get.

This whole matter of owing people money can get pitifully out of hand. Recently a woman approached a financial counselor in Cincinnati asking for help in getting out of debt. She handed over a stack of bills which the counselor added on her desk calculator: department store, $843; another store, $621; finance company, $1,400; installment loan, $3,922; bank credit card, $450. By the time these and other bills had been added, the woman's total debt came to $50,212.

Recent figures indicate that debt payments eat up from twenty to twenty-five percent of the average American's take-home pay. Americans have over 600 million credit cards, an average of over four for each adult in the country. On these they have piled up nearly $500 billion in installment debt. Who but an American would rush to a sale to buy an item at a ten percent discount while letting the carrying charges ride at eighteen percent? Oh, for the good old days when we honored our parents instead of all major credit cards!

Using Credit Cards

Most of us don't really know how to use those little plastic cards that enable us to buy virtually anything just by signing a slip of paper. Credit purchasing is a real science. What is true of wise credit buying today is very different from what was true twenty years ago.

If we go back twenty *centuries*, we find Paul writing to the Romans (13:8), "Owe no debt to anyone except the debt that binds us to love one another. . . ." Today there's plenty of money in our world; the trouble is that everybody owes it to everybody else. Lending money is big business, and our economy would collapse if we all suddenly took Paul's advice. Perhaps, though, that would teach many Americans a lesson. With financial security gone, many might discover that the debt of love can provide wonderful incentive and sustenance.

At the very least we should put more loving concern into our borrowing. We should be less covetous of material items which are beyond our means but which are available because we can buy now and pay later. Wise use of credit is essential in the stewardship of financial resources.

My own preference has been to pay off all credit card purchases at the end of each month. For the most part, the items we have had to pay interest on have been limited to our home mortgage and our automobiles. From a purely economic viewpoint, this was not the soundest possible use of credit. With today's rates of inflation, it would be even less sound to adhere rigidly to this style of credit buying.

What our restricted use of credit *has* done is keep us from buying many things we don't need. We have not run the risk of forgetting the connection between signing the charge slip and having to pay the bill. We have kept our credit cards to a minimum (credit counselors advise carrying no more than two). We have kept aware of how much money we owe and avoided the trap of underestimating the real cost of items that are paid for by installments.

Some credit counselors advise never charging any item that costs less than $25. Paying cash for less expensive items will help you avoid the credit burden that comes with having the small purchases pile up. Paying for a winter coat in the summer may hurt slightly, but you can at least see and feel what you're getting for the money. Small items you could have done without may be used up before they are paid for.

Advantages of Credit

An even sounder economic approach today is to compare what you spend on interest charges with what you save through inflation. Your inflationary savings result from buying the item while it costs less even though you have not accumulated sufficient cash. For example, if you take six months to pay for a new refrigerator and in the process add $20 interest to the cost of the appliance, compare this with the six-month price increase of the refrigerator due to inflation. At the present inflationary rate, you'll probably end up saving money by buying the appliance on credit.

Credit also makes it possible to take better advantage of sales. If you really need an item that is on sale, you don't have to pass up the item because your budget is running low in that particular month.

Another advantage of the availability of credit is a better use of your savings. Consider that most credit cards and charge accounts enable you to get from six to eight weeks of free credit by timing your purchases carefully. If you buy just after the billing date and pay just before the due date, no interest charges are added, and you have free money for almost two months. Even when you incur finance charges on your credit purchases, these charges are tax deductible.

Meantime, your own savings can be accumulating interest—often at a rate that exceeds the interest rate on your credit accounts.

Many businesses are making it difficult to get by without credit cards. To rent a car often requires a credit card for identification, while using a check in a department store must be supported by a driver's license and a credit card.

Borrowing

From time to time, nearly every one of us has to borrow some amount of money. Let's finish this chapter with a few basic principles of sound borrowing.

1. Borrow as little as you can get by with for as short a time as possible. Even though inflation sometimes leads to the possibility of profiting by paying off a loan more slowly, there's a lot to be said for paying back what you owe as quickly as possible.
2. Know exactly what your loan will cost you. Understand the annual percentage rate of interest and what it will translate to in dollars. Steer clear of the small loan company with high interest rates.
3. If you have a loan on your automobile, drive the car at least a year longer than the loan runs. During that time, you can set aside the amount of the payment so that when you have to buy a new car, you will have some cash to add to the trade-in value of your old vehicle.
4. When you need to borrow money, one of the best places to look for a low-cost loan is your life insurance policy. Most ordinary policies make it possible to borrow against cash build-up at a very low rate of interest. Many people take advantage of this low interest rate to invest what they borrow in a reasonably secure stock or in property. Insurance loans are generally repaid upon

the death of the insured by subtracting the amount of the loan from the benefit to the beneficiary.

5. Two other possibilities for low-interest loans are bank passbook loans and short-term unsecured notes. With a bank passbook loan, you are really using your own money, but the loan insures that you will put it back into your savings account within a specified period of time. The short-term unsecured note is a simple interest loan that is paid back in one lump sum. This is the least expensive way to pay interest. Banks sometimes issue such notes to their preferred customers.

6. Borrowing money should never be a response to a whim. One of the great tragedies of our society-run-on-credit is that we tend to incur financial obligations without any real thought. What we should do is ask the Lord's guidance in this important aspect of financial resource use. There should be times when we decide to do without something we'd like to have rather than going more deeply into debt. If we work to control our use of credit, perhaps we can again begin to look forward to the daily visit from the postman.

7

When Your Ship Comes in, It's Always Docked by the Government

It is often said that only two things are inevitable, death and taxes. Sometimes you may find yourself wishing they would come in that order. At least death doesn't get worse each time Congress meets!

How would you like to be faced with both death and taxes at the same time? It happened to a Philadelphia man. The city solicitor's office threatened court action when they found the man owed $5.35 in delinquent taxes. When they discovered that the man was in prison awaiting execution, they decided to drop the case.

Form 1040

April 15 is the income tax deadline. You have a choice: Pay your taxes in due time or do time.

Sitting down with the notorious 1040 is a task most of us defer as long as possible. We're unhappy about the fact that, after we've saved for a rainy day, the government comes along and soaks us. We like Washington's face on our money, but we don't like Washington's hands on it.

Sometime ago a woman on a radio quiz show won a two-family house. She was understandably excited until someone told her that she had to pay taxes on her prize. Knowing that she couldn't raise enough cash to meet this payment, she wrote to the Internal Revenue Service, "You fellows take the lower floor, and let me keep the upper floor."

Another problem is that the income tax form seems to get more complicated every year. Maybe you've had the experience of taking home a handful of 1040s just to be safe in case you spoiled some. One was for the rough draft and all the erasures. On the seventh correction you rubbed a hole through line 18 on page 2 (line 16 less line 17). Fortunately, you had another form to fall back on. Somehow, though, as you were in the middle of copying the figures from the original form, you were interrupted. You could never locate that form again.

The third try went better. You managed to copy all the previous information and figure the balance accurately. Then you were ready to transfer all this data to the final form.

If it hadn't been for that scratchy ball point pen, you might have made it. It's puzzling why there's never a good pen around when you need one most. Impatiently trying to get this one to start writing, you scratched a hole in one of the forms. Then the pen started writing—in blobs.

Perhaps that's when you made the decision to go to H & R Block. It is simpler for a lot of us to get an accountant or a tax expert to prepare our 1040s. What the USA doesn't get, the CPA does. Have you ever wondered what kind of sadistic bent motivates people to go into this means of earning a living?

Saving on Taxes

Nevertheless, our tax bills can be reduced, at least to the minimum required by law. As we carry out our responsibility to support the government, we should be trying to avoid overpayment of taxes. This is just one more reasonable part of our total effort to use our resources well.

Each year, over a million persons who file federal income

tax returns overpay on the basis of the information included on the forms. Countless others overpay by failing to take advantage of tax-saving opportunities. You can avoid costly mistakes and oversights by gaining some knowledge about taxes. This is true even if you have your return prepared by a professional. The knowledge you gain will help you keep adequate records, present your case intelligently to your advisor, and evaluate the advice you receive.

This is not to say you need to know everything there is to know about tax. At the very least, though, study the instruction booklet that comes with the tax returns and get answers to questions you have about it. Think carefully about the categories of allowable deductions and how they apply to your income.

In a real sense, the dollar you save on taxes is worth more than any other dollar you earn. Take any hundred dollars of your income, for example. Depending on your tax bracket, federal taxes might shrink that hundred to fifty dollars or less. State and local taxes would further reduce it. If you can legitimately avoid paying some of these taxes, the savings is worth more than the original hundred dollars. It does not incur new taxation. You might say that a tax-saved dollar buys twice.

What are the best ways you can use to save money on your federal income tax? First of all, let me point out emphatically that cheating is not one of them. Christians are a holy people, and holy people do not lie or steal no matter what "rationale" the Enemy may plant in our minds. When I was a child we had a sing-song saying that went, "Cheatin' shows and never goes." Because we believe in a just God, we know that that's one of those childhood truths that endure forever. But after seeing the career of a friend of mine virtually ruined because he failed to report income, I am also keenly aware that the temporal consequences of income tax dishonesty can be severe.

Three Stages of Tax Savings

On the other hand, there are many completely honest ways for you to avoid paying more than your share of federal income taxes. These can be applied in a three-stage process, the first of which is a year-round, record-keeping system that will insure accuracy, provide valuable documentation, and enable you to save at declaration time. The second stage is end-of-year tax activity to take advantage of available savings opportunities. And, finally, the third stage is pulling together your figures without missing the deductions you have coming.

In the *first stage*, you need to keep track of tax deductions *as they occur*. Promptly place the bills you have paid and the cancelled checks in separate folders or envelopes according to the tax subject. A record of bills paid for such major purchases as furniture, automobiles, and large appliances is essential. Keep records of money spent for the support of dependents not living with you and of personal expenditures that are partly for business purposes. The best time to sort out your bills is when you pay them. The best time to sort out your checks is just after you review your monthly bank statement.

An ongoing diary for recording business expenses might also be a good idea. Expenses for travel and entertainment not reimbursed by your employer should be recorded here. This documentation will be important if you are asked by the IRS to substantiate such expenditures.

We usually think of end-of-year tax saving devices as applicable only to business corporations or the very wealthy. Most of them are. Nevertheless, there are a few end-of-year strategies worth consideration by the individual taxpayer at *stage two*.

For example, if your annual itemized deductions do not exceed the standard deduction allowed each year and for this reason you use the short form, you might check the possibility of bunching your deductions into one year and using the long form on an alternate-year basis. Here's how this would work. You might start with a year in which your itemized deductions will be close to or exceed the amount of the standard deduction. Pay all possible tax-deductible bills on or before December 31 and itemize your deductions for that year. The next year defer payment of tax-deductible items as much as possible until the year after. Then the third year start the cycle all over again.

Deductions can also be shifted into the year when you expect a higher income. Or you might be able to shift your income into a year in which you expect higher deductions. The income-shifting strategy is applicable if you have investments or a business of your own.

The *third stage* of the tax-saving strategy is pulling together your annual figures without overlooking deductions you're entitled to. Let me spell out a few of the most commonly overlooked deductions:

1. Certain medical expenses, including the cost of travel to and from the doctor's office, and medical payment for dependents who do not qualify as tax exemptions.
2. Varied interest charges such as those included in your monthly mortgage payment or your monthly charge account bill.
3. Charitable contributions, including expenses you incur doing volunteer work or gifts of clothing or furniture to a charitable organization.
4. Deductible taxes, including state taxes on retail sales, gasoline taxes, real estate taxes, and personal property taxes.

You do have to be reasonable in listing your deductions. Some years ago, a taxpayer claimed a deduction on a state income tax return for trying to conserve water during a dry spell. As expenses he listed two quarts of blackberry wine a week and two quarts of gin a month. (His claim was rejected.)

On the other hand, a grocer in Albany, New York, claimed and was granted a legitimate business deduction of $37.62 for cat food. He used the cats to catch the mice in his store.

Even the tax experts differ among themselves in interpreting the law. An assemblyman in New York visited eight tax experts and compared their answers about how he stood with the government. He got eight different answers. Several of the experts told him he was entitled to a refund—their estimates ranged from $1,100 to $241. Several others said he owed the government from $149 to $375.

Tax Shelters

Legitimate deductions aside, there are various kinds of tax shelters that can lessen the amount you pay the federal government. For the wealthy among us, the most common and most beneficial forms of tax shelter are certain types of investment. Brokerage firms can provide information on shelters available through gas and oil investments. Occasionally these shelters are available for subscriptions of less than $2000, but usually require $5000 or more.

Real estate is also a good option. The most popular real estate shelter is the multi-family apartment complex. Shelters can also be obtained through investments in warehouses, trailer parks, shopping malls, office buildings, and other forms of real estate.

Even people in low-income tax brackets may be able to save a substantial amount every year in shelters that are relatively free of risk. Examples are the IRA and Keogh plans for workers whose income is not included in a retirement system.

Another possibility is switching the earnings on one's assets to other beneficiaries who are in a much lower tax bracket. This type of trust arrangement must last over ten years or until the death of the beneficiary. You can retain ownership of the assets even while someone else is acquiring the earnings.

Avoiding Income Tax Audits

The prospect of an income tax audit is somewhat traumatic for most of us. We're not particularly afraid that the audit will prove us dishonest or result in our having to pay vastly increased taxes. We do wonder, though, whether we can resurrect the documentation to support all our deductions and whether we can really count on the auditor to give us a "fair shake."

Let's suppose that you want to reduce the chances of an income tax audit. How do you go about it?

The most basic principle is being completely honest. Never fail to report any of your income, no matter how small. The IRS computer will match withholding and information statements from employers and financial institutions with the items reported on your return. If there is any discrepancy, your return could be questioned.

The 1040 form should be filled out in complete detail, with name, address, and social security number accurately provided. You must check the correct blocks indicating filing status and personal exemptions. Using the correct income tax table or rate schedule will help you avoid error, as will checking that all other required information is recorded.

Certain kinds of deductions are more likely to raise questions than others. For example, casualty loss and theft deductions are often open to estimate and could call attention to your return. The same is true of very large amounts claimed for charitable contributions, for travel and entertainment expenses, and for bad debts. You will also be more likely to be audited if you show an increase in the number of exemptions that is unusual for your family's status, or if your 1040 calls for a sizable refund.

It's Easier for a Rich Man to Enter Heaven

The buck really stops at the tax collector's office. With the exception of Matthew the apostle (and he was *converted,* remember!), tax collectors have a lousy reputation. We unfairly describe the IRS as a collection of heartless individuals determined to do us in. One father explained to his daughter that he couldn't afford to buy her a pony because of tax bills. She wrote to the IRS director asking, "Please do not make my father pay income tax just for one week so he can buy me a pony." The letter went from Washington back to regional headquarters in Philadelphia. There six staff members chipped in and bought the girl a pony.

Real Estate Taxes

The New York City Tax Department sends annual property tax bills to the owners of all buildings in the city. Since universities and hospitals are exempt from property taxes, the New York University Medical Center disregarded the billing. The tax collector automatically initiated a repossession action in court, though fortunately the matter was resolved without loss to the Medical Center.

Private citizens aren't always that lucky. You should know that numerous errors occur in determining the rates of real estate tax assessment. Some familiarity with these mistakes might help you determine whether you are being taxed fairly and, if not, whether to make an appeal.

Most errors can be called assessment recording errors. These include arithmetical errors in land and building computations, inaccurate descriptions of the land or the building, failure to record factors that depreciate property value, and inaccurate records of improvements.

Mistakes are also made in overassessing property. Sometimes property is assessed at more than its market value or higher than the legal standard for a given class of property. Assessments may be higher than the legal average for the district or higher than similar properties in the area.

A number of miscellaneous assessment errors also occur, such as improper classification of property or the inclusion of maintenance items as improvements. Any of these errors can provide the basis for an appeal that might result in having your real estate taxes lowered.

Improving the Government

Besides trying to save on our taxes, we can get more for our money by working to improve our government. We complain extensively about the government but feel powerless to improve it. There are actions, however, every one of us can undertake to make it more effective. We owe our efforts to this cause, of course, regardless of our financial resources, since our government affects many areas of our lives. Laws enacted by the legislature limit our freedom while they protect our rights. Decisions made at various governmental levels influence our life-style, our economy, and all other facets of democratic living.

One way to have an influence on government is to become a part of it. Many dedicated Christians have turned their backs on more lucrative careers to enter politics and improve the quality of local, state, and national government.

A career in politics offers a continuous challenge to influence the quality of life in our "one nation under God." Legislators and judges can work to insure that we are governed by laws that are moral and just. Prosecutors and public defenders, councilmen and administrators, diplomats and ambassadors—many forms of governmental service beckon to qualified Christians as fertile opportunities to serve.

There are, of course, aggravations that go with the challenge. The petty annoyances of political campaigning, for example, are reflected in an itemized list of expenses submitted by an unsuccessful contender for county commissioner in Indiana. As part of his expense listing, the candidate included three bottles of aspirin, 125 cups of coffee he bought for others, and a can of ointment "for a burned finger suffered while frying pancakes at a rally."

For most of us, participation in government will be more indirect. Even if we can't be active in a political party, we can support worthwhile candidates. Aggressively working to promote worthwhile issues is commendable, but so is providing others with accurate, objective information concerning candidates and issues.

A very important way each of us has to improve government is through our vote. Whenever a politician promises a pie in the sky, remember whose dough he's planning to use. Each of us has an obligation to be an informed and conscientious voter. I believe we displease God when we treat too lightly this precious opportunity to exercise our freedom. Millions of Americans just don't bother to vote or else cast their votes without understanding the candidates' stands.

A West Coast mayor was concerned some years ago about the apathy of the public toward candidates and set out to prove that few people really care about their votes. He launched a promotional campaign for a city council candidate named Boston Curtis. Curtis won the election. The next day, the mayor announced to the people of the town that they had elected a mule to city council. (And I thought *our* council was stubborn!)

Vote intelligently and encourage others to do likewise. Especially important are local and primary elections. Few politicians reach the national level without starting locally. Choosing the right people for these lesser offices increases the likelihood of effective national government.

Writing to Congressmen

Letters to congressmen can also help to shape more effective government. But these must be intelligent letters expressing an honest point of view. A Sacramento, California, student took a short cut in a class-assigned project of writing letters to congressmen. He mimeographed a short letter and sent it off to twenty-five legislators. Because the content of the letter had not been assigned, the student's message read: "To whoever opens this letter: This letter is to fulfill a requirement for a school course. Please disregard."

Here are a few suggestions about effectively communicating with your congressmen:

1. Be brief, even if the subject is complex. Two pages is one too many.
2. State your own views. Indicate why you feel as you do about any piece of legislation or other governmental action.
3. Make it plain which of the thousands of bills introduced each year you are referring to.
4. Write in time to influence your congressman's vote— preferably before the bill is out of committee.
5. Avoid threats or promises.
6. Address the letter correctly.

Our government, like all other human endeavors, can be improved. There are thousands of small changes which will actually save significant amounts of money. Some years ago, for example, the Administrative Management Society honored a customs official for cutting down on superfluous paperwork. As assistant director of inspection and control, the aide had eliminated eighty-nine governmental forms at a savings of over $340,000 a year.

I believe we should be honest about the weak spots in our government, but not overemphasize them. Our time and energy should be spent building up, not tearing down. Help people become aware of what they owe their country, rather than what their country owes them. The emphasis should be on obligations and responsibilities rather than always on personal rights.

Running a government as vast as ours involves many complicated problems. Oversimplifying is easy, as is jumping to conclusions without careful study of the facts. We call our government incompetent. We criticize our leaders. We encourage those who would cast authority aside. Our attitudes toward authority leave much room for improvement.

The most important point of all is to accept the source of government authority as God Himself. Every time we obey a law out of a sense of responsibility, we are showing reverence for God's authority over us. Even as we seek to promote good and just government for all people, we must realize that it is ultimately by prayer rather than by politics that a better world can be brought into being. The transformation can take place only through travail, through the suffering of good men becoming better, through the dedication of mankind to a cause that transcends each of us as well as our individual rights and responsibilities.

Don't prove disloyal and weak by starting out to improve society, only to fall back when the suffering begins. Being willing to give up our pride and comfort keeps us open to the redeeming, creative power of the Holy Spirit in the guiding of our personal and community lives.

Here, then, is a summary of ways an individual can help improve the way he is governed:

1. Participate directly through a career in politics or governmental work.
2. Encourage other God-fearing persons to enter governmental careers.
3. Join worthwhile civic groups and actively participate.
4. Keep up to date on candidates and issues in local, state, and national government.
5. Register and vote in primary, state, and national elections.
6. Follow newspaper reports of how your congressmen vote on various legislation.
7. Know your congressmen and let them be informed of your opinions.

8. Know and make your voice heard by local officials, councilmen, etc.
9. Ask the Lord for generous blessings for our country and offer yourself to be used as He sees fit.

8

My Doctor Writes His Prescriptions in Illegible Latin, But His Bills Are in Plain English

Medical science has come a long way. I understand some surgeons are now billing separately for labor and parts. Indeed recent advances in medical practice have been so far reaching that it's now almost impossible for a doctor *not* to find something wrong with you. Most of our ailments are the same as they were a hundred years ago, only they now have more expensive names.

Even those of us who are blessed with good health usually find that safeguarding that blessing takes a sizable chunk from our financial resources. Doctor's bills, hospital bills, medical insurance premiums, medicine costs, bills from optometrists, bills from dentists, bills from pediatricians and other specialists—it's enough to drive you to the psychiatrist, where you find out what big bills really look like.

Some of us have difficulty getting all these bills paid. Dr. R. J. Shull delivered a baby in 1910 and received payment for the service in 1953. He was seventy-five years old when he received a long-distance phone call from the woman asking how much she owed him. The doctor replied that he couldn't recall the amount due and suggested that the lady forget about the bill. Her sense of responsibility persisted, however, and she airmailed him a check for $50.

Doctor God

Benjamin Franklin once said, "God heals, and the doctor takes the fees." That, of course, is as it should be. God

94

doesn't need the money, after all. God doesn't need us either, but He chooses to work through us.

Sometime back I was standing on a street corner downtown waiting for the light to change. I overheard two people discussing what would happen if they suddenly became very ill. "Which would you ask for first, a priest or a doctor?" one asked.

"I'd ask for the doctor," the other replied. "Then I might not need the priest."

Religion is too often perceived as a kind of last resort. When things go well, we seldom think of our constant dependence on God's help. We behave like the woman passenger on an ocean liner during a storm. Nervously she asked the captain, "Are we in great danger?"

"Don't worry," the captain replied. "After all, we're in the hands of God."

"Oh!" the woman gasped in terror. "Is it really that bad?"

As we use the various medical services available to us, we need to keep the right perspective. God's loving hands surround us at all times. He can cure our every ill, just as Jesus enabled the blind to see, the lame to walk—yes, even the dead to live—while He was on earth. But the Lord has given us medical science and its practitioners as the usual means through which He brings His power to bear on us physically. The vast majority of Christians believe that using a portion of our financial resources for medical services is part of God's plan for our lives. Nothing is taken away from the fundamental Source of these and all our other benefits.

Unusual cures are often called miracles. If relief from a physical ailment is beyond the projected capabilities of medical science, we feel another Hand has been at work. It should not be difficult for a Christian to believe in miracles. We should, however, understand what a miracle really is. Believing miracles are temporary suspensions of God's law gets in the way of our understanding God's true strength. More accurately, miracles represent a transcending of God's laws *as we know and understand them*. In other words, a miracle is as much in accord with God's law as an ordinary dawn or sunset. It is an event that God sends into our lives to reveal His laws that we have not yet understood. To deny the possibility of miracles according to this definition would be to limit God to the laws we understand. God Himself is miraculous, and this fact alone compels us to believe that He has laws beyond our understanding.

Augustine wrote, "Miracles do not happen in contradiction to nature, but only in contradiction to that which is known to us about nature." There is so much we don't know! Our understanding of God's ways is so limited that we can only stand in awe of His omnipotence.

And yet He wants to move us toward better understanding. When we meet Him face to face, all the distortions and shadows of our present understanding will be taken away. Each of us will be filled and transformed by this union with Him in perfect understanding. For now, we seek glimmers of insight into the reasons for what happens to us. With each inspired insight, we are able to see our relationship to God in a more meaningful way.

The hand of God is no less at work in relieving us of the simplest headache. In His love, He is always concerned with our welfare, both physical and spiritual. Illness and disease enter our lives only as He can use them to bring us closer to Him. And always He will relieve us of the burden of our physical ailments, through natural or supernatural means, as soon as a return to health is in our best interests.

If we are open to His grace, we will receive a continuous supply of strength and vitality through the working of the Holy Spirit. The effect of this power within us Paul described to the Romans: "If the Spirit of him who raised Jesus from the dead dwells in you, then he who raised Christ from the dead will bring your mortal bodies to life also, through His Spirit dwelling in you" (8:11).

An outstanding modern example of this kind of working of the Holy Spirit is Corrie Ten Boom. In World War II, the

My Doctor Writes His Prescriptions

Ten Boom family harbored a number of Jews to protect them from the Nazi massacre. Eventually the family was taken captive and placed in a concentration camp. Of the members of her family, only Corrie survived the long imprisonment. She came through the experience with a vitality that gives eloquent testimony of the power of the Holy Spirit within us.

Maintaining Good Health

Certainly the Lord wants us to take care of our bodies. Nearly every one of us has had some formal education in how to do this. The primary question to be discussed here is how we can *afford* to do it.

First we can cut certain spending habits. Some things we spend our money on not only represent areas of possible savings, but also hinder our health. Obvious examples are smoking and recreational activities that cause serious loss of sleep.

Health researchers have established seven significant habits that contribute to better health and longer lives. These are:

1. Getting moderate exercise
2. Maintaining proper weight
3. Getting eight hours of sleep every night
4. Eating breakfast daily
5. Not eating snack foods
6. Not smoking
7. Drinking only in moderation.

Research shows that persons who follow six or seven of the above live significantly longer than those who follow three or fewer. The health of those who practice these habits is, on the average, as good as that of persons twenty years younger who live less regulated lives.

Hypochondriacs

Another way you could save a lot of money is by getting rid of all the hypochondriacs in your family. A good portion of the money spent on medical bills is wasted because there was really nothing physically wrong in the first place. Most of us have some impulse, from self-pity or other motive, to complain to others about our aches and pains. That's the trouble with laryngitis. You can't tell anybody about it until you've recovered.

Most of us, too, can recognize that how we feel physically is strongly influenced by our mental attitudes and outlook. The influence of our minds over our bodies can be very powerful. Not long ago the *British Medical Journal* reported the case of what must be history's most extreme hypochondriac. Over a thirty-four-year period, the patient had been hospitalized on at least two hundred occasions. He received hundreds of X-rays and thousands of blood tests. His abdomen looked like a scarred battlefield as a result of the many operations performed on him. Over this period of time, the medical costs of this single patient totaled $2 million. Not once did doctors find anything really wrong with him.

Our minds can also help us feel better. Recognizing this, doctors sometimes give patients placebos, pills made from harmless ingredients like bread or sugar. Some patients get well, or at least start feeling better, while taking placebos merely because they think they are taking a drug and expect it to work.

Some years ago an American manufacturer managed to produce iodine that was completely without sting. The company expected the product to be tremendously successful. Sales started to rise, but then fell off suddenly. A study the company commissioned found that people believed iodine had to hurt and sting in order to work well. As a result, the manufacturer added an ingredient to its product just to make it hurt again.

Our Age of Alleviation

Ours is an age of alleviation. We have medicines and remedies for almost everything, with man's scientific expertise still discovering ways of bringing relief from a variety of physical ailments. Having the means available to get rid of suffering frees us to choose not to use the remedy, but instead to suffer with Christ. Our crucified Lord had a remedy always available: A mere act of the will would have freed Him from His tormentors. He chose instead to give Himself totally to our redemption.

We are never wrong to ask that suffering be removed from our lives or that we be permitted to avoid a painful experience. The catch is our pleas must always be accompanied by wholehearted acceptance of God's will. Sometimes we *must* deal with pain and suffering head-on. Otherwise, we become like children who have been overmedicated against childhood diseases and have never built an immunity. Clearly, there is a valid place in life for suffering, not for its own sake but because it purges our souls in a way that nothing else can.

Someone who never has to fight to maintain his equanimity in the midst of suffering misses an important opportunity for growth. He may never know the full meaning of friendship, derived not from joyful moments of celebration but rather from times of anguish shared by human hearts in unison. A full appreciation of the beauty of life comes only as one can look steadily into the face of death.

By no means does this imply that we should cease all attempts to lessen pain. Particularly where others are concerned, we need to continue to bring comfort and relief. In our own lives, too, we can justifiably seek freedom from pain if for no other reason than that if healthy we are better able to perform our duties and be of service to fellow human beings. It is just that we should not be afraid of suffering when it is inevitable, nor spend all our effort avoiding it.

Our country is extremely pain-conscious. Moved by a barrage of commercial advertising, we grab available medication or trot off to the doctor for the slightest pain. Instilled in our thinking is the belief that any trace of pain is to be quickly banned as an intolerable evil. If you believe in the law of supply and demand, how can you explain why there are more kinds of headache remedies than headaches?

Doctors' offices are filled with people alarmed by insignificant pain and morbidly convinced their ailments are much more serious than they really are. Doctors spend too much of their time dealing with trivial pain and do not have enough time to give to those genuinely in need of treatment.

Keeping the Patient Away

Personally, although I have great faith in our family doctor, I see him very seldom. (Every time I go, he tells me that if I don't cut something out, he will.) Many parents call the doctor as soon as a child runs a temperature. Many kids are very good at running temperatures on days when they don't feel like going to school. There is much to say for the good old days when the best healer was time.

Now you might think that's strong advice coming from a man who collects money from people who bring him problems. Actually I do encourage people to work out their own emotional and psychological difficulties. If I really thought many people would follow the advice to its extreme, I might be more cautious.

One physician offers these guidelines for cutting medical expenses in half:

1. Remember that colds and flu have no known cures. Aspirin, rest, and fluids are the best treatment of symptoms.
2. You can treat minor bruises and cuts by cleaning well with soap and water and applying a bandage. For minor infection, just use a mild antiseptic.
3. Understand that occasional headaches are normal. Try

a combination of aspirin and rest, and heat the neck muscles to ease the pressure.

4. Heat and rest will also heal sprains and strains. Your doctor has no magical cure to speed up the mending of such problems.

5. Nearly all backaches are due to muscle strain. Aspirin and heat will ease the pain.

6. Minor puncture wounds almost never require a visit to the doctor. If you have had a recent tetanus booster, just swab the spot with alcohol or iodine.

7. Do-it-yourself medical guides are useful in instructing you how to treat minor problems and evaluate symptoms.

The ability to evaluate your own symptoms realistically is important. Get to know your body's distress signals and find out what they mean. You can develop a good sense of when medical attention is really necessary. Treating a hacking cough unsuccessfully for three weeks with over-the-counter cough preparation, for instance, can be far more costly in the long run than seeing your doctor quickly.

Saving on Medicine

If we're careful not to overdo it, we can treat many of our minor physical ailments without danger. Ordinary drugs bought without prescription will ease many of the symptoms that interfere with functioning effectively in God's service.

Of the vast array of these over-the-counter drugs, aspirin is the most commonly used. A safe and effective pain-killer for headaches, aching muscles, and rheumatic pain, it also eases flu and cold symptoms and brings down fever. The best buy in aspirin is usually the least expensive product available. Aspirin itself is standardized and extra ingredients that increase the price don't change its basic effectiveness.

Nor is it necessarily good economy to buy in large quantities. Moisture and heat can cause chemical decomposition, which reduces aspirin's effectiveness and increases the likelihood of stomach irritation. Your best bet is to buy the amount you are likely to use within a few months.

Other kinds of over-the-counter drugs sometimes have value but need to be used with care. Never take a drug unless you need it. Frequent use of non-prescription remedies makes them less effective. Always follow directions on the label, and never combine several drugs without telling your doctor what you're doing.

The advice of a physician is sometimes crucial in choosing remedies for an ailment. If we remember that over-the-counter drugs are never intended to prevent or cure illness or infections, but merely to relieve their symptoms, we'll be more likely to seek the doctor's advice when we need it.

If your doctor gives you a prescription, don't try to read it. There's no course in cryptography in the world that will make it possible for you to decode what your doctor writes on that prescription form. I heard of one doctor who ran into bad times and tried to rob a bank. Unfortunately, nobody could read his holdup note.

Sometimes I worry about whether even the pharmacist can read the doctor's handwriting. What would happen if he gave the wrong prescription? A Tallahassee man had an experience somewhat like that. It seems the druggist reversed the labels on two prescriptions that he had brought in simultaneously. The patient claimed the result was that he had been rubbing stomach medicine on his scalp and taking a tablespoon of hair tonic three times a day after meals.

The doctor will sometimes prescribe a drug known to be effective in treating a given condition. The price variations in over-the-counter medications are magnified where prescription drugs are concerned. One government study showed the price range for a single drug as being $16.50 to $2.95. Obviously it's important to do some comparison shopping before having your prescription filled. Competitive pricing of prescription drugs is becoming common.

The price, of course, is not the only consideration. The same drug might vary in quality from one manufacturer to another. This is difficult for the consumer to assess, but your physician will be able to help. Sometimes he will suggest a certain brand rather than giving a generic prescription.

Similarly you may choose to stay with the druggist you have dealt with for years even though his prices are somewhat higher. Convenience and service are important factors. However, if you have price information, you can make an informed choice. Choosing a pharmacist who charges more for prescriptions means you can expect additional service or convenience.

Cutting Medical Bills

Here are eleven other ideas for trimming your medical expenses while safeguarding your health:

1. Locate a family doctor before illness strikes. Despite all the jokes about the time doctors spend on the golf course, most general practitioners are busy people. If someone they have never served telephones for help, they may or may not have time to see the patient.

2. Anytime you select a new doctor, ask him to have your old doctor forward all of your family's medical records. These records will be a guide to quicker, more accurate diagnoses and will prevent duplication of tests and immunizations.

3. Discuss fees before you run up a bill. Having some concept of what a visit to the doctor's office will cost will help you judge the wisdom of seeking help for less serious needs. Doctors are not likely to inquire about your finances on their own, but many are willing to lower their basic fees for persons of limited means.

4. Have regular checkups. To try to save by bypassing periodic physical examinations is foolish. Even the

examination that reveals no hint of illness is worth everything it costs. You'll have greater peace of mind knowing that you are well. Even more importantly, you can save your life by detecting serious illness early or at least avoid the enormous expense of doctor, drug, and hospital bills that are linked with the advanced stages of many ailments.

5. There are several things you can do to keep the cost of hospitalization down. First you can sometimes reduce the number of days of confinement by arranging tests to be conducted on an outpatient basis. By having the tests completed before admission, you can return home until the results are ready and then be checked in for surgery.

6. Once you know that you are to be hospitalized, check your health insurance to clarify the extent of coverage. Find out whether you are eligible for state or federal assistance. Knowing what kind of coverage you have will prevent the agony of being handed a bill that you have no means of paying.

7. Ask your doctor about a choice of hospitals. He may be able to select a hospital that will be best for you and least expensive. Community hospitals will save you money over large medical centers and university hospitals. You won't get the same quality of service, of course, but in many cases the savings will more than justify this sacrifice. If you are likely to be hospitalized for some time, it is often wise to enter a hospital that has progressive patient care. In such situations patients are moved to less expensive quarters when they no longer need constant attention.

8. It's a good idea to ask your doctor whether the hospital has a special unit for which you qualify. Examples are self-care units and one-day outpatient surgery units. Treatment in such facilities will usually be less expensive.

9. Let your doctor know that you do not wish to stay in the hospital any longer than absolutely necessary. It might be possible for you to transfer to a nursing facility where the expenses will be less.

10. Ask yourself whether you really need that private room. The choice of a private room is sometimes more a matter of prestige or comfort than real patient benefit. Often it results in paying higher fees to medical personnel who charge on the basis of what the patient seems able to afford.

11. At the time of discharge from the hospital, check the bill carefully. If you feel you have been overcharged, raise a question immediately. Delaying will make it more difficult to obtain satisfaction.

9

Yesterday I Took the Car to the Garage for Four Shocks, and Ended Up With Five

The self-serve gasoline pumps at most stations now have detailed directions for operation. You may have wondered why anyone who has driven awhile and observed attendants filling gas tanks would need such step-by-step guidance. Well, I'm not sure where it happened, but in one station a woman drove up to a pump, got out of her car, opened her gas tank, and lifted the hose from the pump. Then, somewhat puzzled, she stuck a dollar bill into the nozzle of the hose. When nothing happened, she tried shouting her gasoline order into the nozzle.

Self-service is a way of saving a few pennies a gallon on gasoline, a trimming of costs many of us take advantage of. This still doesn't soften the shock when we first realize how much we are spending on transportation. As families move to the suburbs, the amount of money required for transportation is constantly increasing. Add to the greater distance the spiraling cost of fuel and of automobiles themselves, and transportation becomes a significant aspect of budgetary planning. One big problem is how to find out how many miles you get to a gallon when you can never afford to fill the tank.

Our plan to meet transportation costs must include operation and upkeep. Costs should be calculated not only for fuel, but also for repair, replacement of parts, licenses, insurance, service, and depreciation. Usual transportation expenditures in a family with one working member and one car amount to about ten percent of the family budget.

Yesterday I Took the Car to the Garage

I'm old enough to remember when $300 was the down payment on a new car, not the sales tax. Back then many cars used to stop on a dime. Now they won't even start on one. Fuel costs have risen to the point where you almost have to turn over the title to your car just to pay for the gas.

Buying a Car

Let's look first at the cars themselves. In recent years, the automobile industry has stopped adding options to new cars. Now they just add to the price tag. If you buy a *used* car, you're very likely to get one that's trouble-free. The trouble comes free with the car.

The decision whether to buy a new or used automobile involves several important considerations. Most of these, however, reduce themselves to two basic questions:

1. How much do you know about cars?
2. How important is it that your car be reliable?

If you know enough about automobiles, you can avoid buying someone else's troubles with his used car. You can check the vehicle thoroughly to make sure it is in good condition before you buy it. Even a well-cared-for older car, though, is more likely to need repair than a new one. Being able to do your own repair work on an automobile is a priceless talent.

Another consideration is that the need for repairs will incapacitate a vehicle from time to time. Sometimes the malfunction occurs when you can least afford it. Again, a new vehicle is likely to be more dependable. If having a certain car in operation is crucial in your life, buying a new car is a better idea.

What is the best approach in selecting an appropriate new automobile? To begin with, it's a good idea to list your needs. What are the main uses you will have for the car—trips to and from work, use in your business, short pleasure drives, long trips? Your answer here should determine the kind of vehicle to shop for. Long trips make a larger car with more horsepower desirable, particularly if gasoline can be written off as a business expense. On the other hand, for a car used in town or for short trips, a compact offers economy, ease of handling, and greater parking flexibility.

Before you choose either a make of car or an agency to buy it from, check the company's reliability in honoring warranties and meeting service obligations. You'll usually be better off choosing an agency close to home so that servicing and checkups won't be a serious inconvenience.

When buying a new car, it often pays to bargain with the salesperson. If you have a trade-in, some bargaining before coming to terms is almost expected. Get yourself a list of manufacturers' suggested retail prices on the models of cars that interest you. Take some extra time for comparison shopping among various dealers.

You're likely to find the best bargains if you shop for your automobile in early fall before the new models are released. This is especially true if you expect to drive the same car for five years or more. Hundreds of dollars can be saved on the purchase, with little or no effect on resale value after a period of time.

New Car Problems

Unfortunately, even a new car seldom runs as smoothly as the salesperson talks. And the dealer who says he stands behind every car he sells is never there when you need a push. As one dissatisfied customer put it, "Cinderella's coach turned into a pumpkin. My dream car turned into a lemon."

Even a reputable company such as General Motors is not above cutting corners at the consumer's expense. In 1977 a Chicago man took his Oldsmobile in for a checkup and found that he had a 350-cubic-inch V-8 engine made by the Chevrolet Motor Car Division under his hood. He went to the attorney general of Illinois and started a movement in which the attorney generals of forty-seven states sued the manufacturer. Because the company had failed to make the substitution of engines a part of their advertising, they had to rebate $200 per car to more than 100,000 persons who had purchased vehicles with that engine.

Next to the atom bomb, the loudest noise in the world is that first rattle in your new car. When you pay the very high price it takes to buy a new automobile these days, you expect perfection. That's understandable, but you won't get it. If the problems that come with your new automobile are relatively minor, count yourself lucky.

An Oakland, California, man couldn't take any more of his unpredictable automobile. When the car broke down one time too many, he picked up a .22 rifle, pumped several shots into the tires, smashed the radiator and spark plugs with a rock, tore out the upholstery, and set fire to the remains. A man in Louisiana who was having trouble with his car also took extreme measures. He had struggled for nearly an hour to get the car started and, over this time, his anger had mounted steadily. At last, he grew so impatient that he got out of the car, found two sticks of dynamite, lit them, and threw them into the vehicle. The explosion scattered parts all over town. Though such remedies get rid of the problem quickly, you're not any closer to getting to work.

Buying a Used Car

If you decide to purchase a secondhand automobile, there are two options you should consider. One is buying from the little old lady who used the car only to get to church and back—or from some other friend you know you can trust. The second best bet is finding an agency offering a guarantee for the first few months of use. Even though only the major parts of the vehicle are covered, you have at least some assurance of quality. One excellent source of used cars is the new car dealer who accepts trade-ins from customers who regularly buy a new car every few years.

Whatever the source of your vehicle, trying it out is a must before laying down good cash. First, let the car idle after you start it, listening for the uneven sounds indicating an expensive tune-up is needed. Check basics such as lights, wipers, and turn signals.

Now press down firmly on the accelerator while the car is in neutral. Look to see whether white or bluish smoke comes out of the exhaust pipe. Such smoke is a sign that the engine is worn and probably won't give good service for long.

Next, check the shocks. Push down on the corners of the car to see whether they bounce back quickly and come to a fast stop. Look to see whether the car sits evenly or whether one corner is lower than the others. This might indicate weak springs.

A coat of paint can cover many problems in a car's body. Look for off colors that might indicate rust underneath.

On the road, see how quietly and smoothly the engine runs. Listen for rattles and check the shock absorbers on rough terrain. Test the brakes to see whether they engage readily without causing the car to swerve toward one side or the other. Look at the tread on the tires and check for uneven wear.

These steps you can follow even if you know very little about automobiles. If you are still unsure, let a trusted mechanic look it over thoroughly. Then take his advice.

Leasing a Car

Many people who use an automobile a great deal for business are turning to leasing rather than buying their cars. Leasing has one major disadvantage. At the end of the lease period, you have nothing to show for your money. On the other hand, you are spared most of the headaches of owning and operating an automobile.

Leasing is virtually free of hassle. The leasing agent will find the kind of car you want. A down payment is unnecessary, but you may have to pay a one-month security deposit.

On the average, leasing payments run about fifteen percent lower than monthly payments on an automobile loan.

A new car depreciates faster than any other asset. By leasing you can have a new car every two or three years and not worry about this depreciation. You'll have a tidy record of your auto expenses and, to the extent that the automobile is used for business purposes, you can write these expenses off on your income tax return.

Whether buying or leasing, it makes sense to get the best possible combination of quality and economy. Buying an expensive car that far exceeds your transportation needs makes no more sense than buying a heap that will not run simply because it's cheap.

In other words, your attempts to save on transportation costs must be reasonable. A mechanic once advised a friend that he could save the $40 cost of a carbon elimination job by driving his car fast for about three or four miles. A little while later the driver was arrested for driving 90 miles an hour. He was fined $90.

Automobile Maintenance

One key to reasonable savings is spending your money on maintenance rather than on repair. Maintenance is preventive care of the car, thus avoiding the need for expensive *corrective* repair. The owner's manual supplied by the manufacturer provides an excellent guide for preventive maintenance. You'll find there schedules for oil changes, oil and gas filter replacement, tune-ups, brake adjustment, checking fluid levels, etc. The more faithful you are in following these guidelines, the less likely it is that you will have expensive repair costs.

A car under warranty must be worked on by an authorized dealer that sells your make of car. Under unusual circumstances you might be able to get approval from the manufacturer's regional office to have someone else do the work. In any case, get to know the service manager and be sure you can be comfortable in trusting your automobile to him.

Self-service gasoline pumps have caused many of us to neglect checking the oil, transmission fluid, brake fluid, power steering fluid, and water in the battery. This lack of attention often proves very costly.

Getting Them Fixed

Inevitably, some repair will be necessary, regardless of how well you care for your car. By the time you need a mechanic you should have established for yourself the best place to take your vehicle. In other words, it's wise to shop around for a reliable repair shop before you need one.

There's no question that getting a good repair job on an automobile at a reasonable cost can be difficult. Virginia Knauer, former Special Assistant for Consumer Affairs, pointed out several years ago that "by far the highest percentage of consumer complaints received in my office each month pertains to automobiles. A common thread seems to run through a great many of them—the problem of servicing."

What can the consumer do?

Get the advice of friends who know something about automobiles before you choose your mechanic. Ask them to recommend a dependable garage. Check consumer complaint records with your Better Business Bureau. One factor to be considered is whether the garage pays its mechanics straight salaries—a much better arrangement for you because it prevents the rush jobs resulting from paying mechanics on a commission basis.

Another valuable source of information is the nonprofit National Institute for Automotive Service Excellence. This group certifies mechanics that have passed proficiency tests, and entrusting your repairs to such a mechanic is likely to improve your service.

Yesterday I Took the Car to the Garage

No matter how carefully you've checked out the garage, you'll still want to be cautious. Never let the service manager talk you into leaving your car without deciding what needs to be done. Never sign a repair order with vaguely worded items such as "tune-up." Have the service writer or mechanic fill in all work that is to be done, the parts to be used, and the labor charges before you sign the repair order. If you aren't sure what needs to be done, have the mechanic go with you for a drive so you can have the specific symptom written on the repair order.

Always insist that the mechanic make no additional repairs without consulting you. Sometimes you'll get a call that will shock you out of your shoes. You've taken the vehicle in for some minor repair and the mechanic telephones with a discovery that will cost you several hundred dollars. Never—repeat, never—let him do that work until you have the opinion of another mechanic.

A Cincinnati man found that it pays to shop around for repairs. When his automobile failed to pass safety inspection because the front end was out of line, he took it to one repair shop. There he was told it needed an alignment plus wheel bearings and new shocks in order to pass inspection. The estimated cost was well over $100. A second mechanic told him that all the car needed was an alignment, which could be done for $14.35. The car then passed the inspection.

Above all, avoid the situation of having to commit yourself to an unfamiliar repair shop because your car has completely broken down, leaving you unable to shop around. It has been estimated that a third of all the money spent for automobile repairs is wasted because of incompetence or dishonesty.

Special Caution

If your automobile breaks down while you have it out of town, you could be at the mercy of unscrupulous garagemen or mechanics. Before taking any extended trips, therefore, it's wise to take the car in for a special check by a mechanic you trust. Have him fix anything that needs repair. Tell your hometown mechanic how many miles you plan to travel and ask him to list the things that might go wrong while you're on the road.

Don't leave your car unattended when you stop at gas stations along the highway. If you need to use the restroom, wait until your car has been serviced and then park near the restroom entrance. If you have the attendant check under the hood, get out of the car and watch what he does. You don't have to know much about what you're watching; the attendant isn't likely to try anything dishonest with your eyes on him.

It's a good idea to pay for any repair work with check or credit card, thus giving you a record of the work done in case some dispute arises. Take old parts with you and have your regular mechanic look at the work that was done. If you become convinced that you were tricked, you may want to write to the garage and try to get your money back.

Complaining

If you have had your car repaired and are displeased with the service, register your complaint immediately. Putting it off even a few days gives the mechanic a chance to think of things that could have caused your problem after you left the garage.

There are civilized, Christian ways to let automobile repairmen know when we are displeased with their work. Sometimes getting satisfaction turns out to be easier than we anticipate. It's usually fastest to make your initial complaint orally. On the other hand, if the problem is not then taken care of right away, be sure to state your complaint in writing.

One defense the mechanic might put forward is that what you are complaining about is normal after what has been

114

done to your car. "It'll work itself out," he may say. "If it doesn't bring the car back and we'll fix it without charge." Such a promise is easily forgotten. Get it in writing.

If your complaint is against a dealership and the service manager does not take care of it, don't hesitate to go directly to the president of the company. In this way you identify yourself as someone who does not give up easily. Be firm in your approach; after all, you aren't asking for any favors. You only want what you paid for.

If your effort to win the cooperation of the president of the dealership is unsuccessful, you might next try calling or writing the zone manager of the manufacturer. Your owner's manual probably lists the addresses of zone managers. Present your case to him and try to arrange for him to look at your car and the problems you are complaining about. Unfortunately, zone managers will often do nothing more than offer a sympathetic form letter noting that the automobile dealer is an independent businessman and that the manufacturer can't control his repair service.

If neither dealer nor zone manager follows through to your satisfaction, write directly to the car manufacturer. Outline your position clearly, but don't make any statements you're not ready to follow through on. That means you may need to make a decision about whether you are ready to take legal action if necessary.

Independent repair shops are often quicker to give satisfaction. Service is ordinarily more personal, making complaints easier to resolve. The independent garageman depends on his customers to advertise his services to their friends and won't want to antagonize you. Usually he will talk to you himself, so don't settle for any of his employees unless you have to. You want the person you talk to to be able to make the decision you need to get fair treatment.

Unsuccessful attempts at settlement could be dealt with by returning to the garage at a time when other customers are around and again presenting your complaint in forceful and audible language. The independent garageman does not want customers to get the idea that he does not care for their best interests. Your chances of winning a case at such a time are considerably improved.

Your next recourse beyond strong words should be the local licensing board or the Independent Garage Owners of America. Since the garage owner needs a permit to operate his shop, he'll want to give satisfactory service to clear his record of standing complaints. The IGOA is a group that exercises strong sanctions against members who fail to live up to their code of ethics.

If this section gives you the impression that it's difficult to get a car fixed, you're right. Consider, for example, how you would go about having your horn repaired. What do you do with a dead horn when you drive up to the door of the repair shop and read the sign, "Blow Horn and Automatic Door Will Open"?

Personally, I haven't had a lot of difficulty getting satisfactory auto repairs. I consider myself especially blessed in view of the age of the cars I drive. One of our automobiles is so old that instead of a dashboard clock it has a sun dial. The last time I took it in for an oil change, the mechanic advised me to keep the oil and change the car.

Parking Problems

There are a lot of other kinds of aggravation associated with automobiles. Take parking, for example. Really, there are plenty of parking places around. The trouble is, they're already taken. Our country averages more than a million major crimes each year, not including double parking. Eventually in desperation you end up parking in a lot. You know what a parking lot is: a place where you leave your car to have your fenders and doors dented.

Comparatively, though, dents are easier to take than some other results of leaving our cars in public places. One unfortunate woman parked her car in an honor system lot and somebody stole it. In London an exasperated motorist gave up looking for a parking spot and left his car parked illegally with the following note on the windshield: "I have circled this block twenty times. I have an appointment to keep. Forgive us our trespasses."

He kept his appointment and returned to his car. There was a new note: "I have circled this block for twenty years. If I don't give you a ticket, I lose my job. Lead us not into temptation."

Auto Accidents

A West Virginia newspaper photographer, fairly new on the job and eager to make a good impression, got in his car and started out on a new assignment. Unfortunately, he became so engrossed in looking around for the pictures he needed that he crashed head-on into a car coming from the opposite direction.

He was understandably embarrassed by the whole incident. But when photographers came and started taking pictures, it greatly increased his chagrin. His assignment, you see, had been to take pictures for traffic safety posters.

I hope you won't mind if this chapter on saving money on automobiles includes this one plea for more attention to saving lives. People today in all walks of life prefer to ride. It's crucial that more of us be content to let the rest of the world go by while we drive within the speed limit. Driving defensively is a must. If all the cars in the world were placed end to end, some character would still pull out and try to pass them. The guy who drives like he owns the road probably doesn't even own the car.

Unfortunately, justice seldom prevails in this life. On a rainy day in San Antonio, a woman stopped suddenly on a highway, and eight cars following her plowed into each other. Traffic was snarled for hours. As the drivers of the

117

eight cars examined the damage to their vehicles, police began issuing traffic citations. They started with the last driver and worked their way forward. Imagine their surprise when they reached the head of the line and found that the driver who had caused all the trouble had driven quietly away.

A Short Digression

This has been a pragmatic chapter, but I'm getting philosophical now. Before I outline some final practical ideas about how to save on fuel costs, a word about slowing down and road maps.

Last year a blizzard hit Cincinnati. This is the second consecutive winter in which new records have been set by the severity of the weather.

In many parts of our country citizens take heavy snowfalls in stride. Snowplows clear the roads, automobiles are equipped to travel under difficult circumstances, and drivers know how to keep their vehicles moving. This has never been true in our city. In the first place, our terrain is very hilly— they say the city is built on seven hills; it must be more like seven hundred. Then, too, our citizens have never really become accustomed to having snow on the ground. Even an inch or so slows everything down.

There's something rather wholesome about this, however. In the recent blizzard, I felt our family life developed additional strength because neither parents nor children were on the move quite so much. At work I heard several people comment to the same effect. One father talked about playing more games with the children than at any other time. A mother said how much she enjoyed saying to her teenagers, "I'm sorry, I just can't take you anywhere now."

Eating lunch at McDonald's one day, I overheard a gentleman report his surprise at seeing a man ice skating down a main thoroughfare, briefcase in hand, on his way to work one

118

morning. His luncheon companion described another symptom of slowing our pace down. He had had a dead battery at the supermarket a day or so earlier. The store manager had made a public address announcement requesting that someone with battery cables come forward. Ten people came forward, eager to help.

There are more rewards to slowing down than safer highways.

Road Maps

Someone defined a road map as the only thing that doesn't fold up after a long drive. I remember the day my wife gave up trying to read road maps. We were driving through the West on a highway that roughly followed the course of a river. On the map Hilda had identified a town in which this highway ran very close to the one we wanted. After driving many miles to reach this town, however, we looked at the map again and realized there was no bridge in the area to get us across the river.

We often misread our maps. Ever since we took that wrong turn in the Garden of Eden, our ability to read maps accurately has lessened. Still, even when we head down the wrong road, if we keep our eyes open we can see the signpost of Christ's cross pointing the way in the right direction toward our eternal destiny. While on that road it is important to remember that maps have a way of being deceptively simple. No hills and valleys, breaks in the pavement, nor newly erected detours show up. There is a similar simplicity in the Ten Commandments. It seems as if it shouldn't be terribly hard to follow only ten road-signs to our destiny. Anyone who takes the journey seriously, however, will soon find that his actual traveling is much more difficult than the map suggests. The terrain is rough.

It's still a problem to me—long after my firm Christian commitment—that the road we must follow is so straight and narrow. I know that the standards and principles that guide my life should be those that are set down in Christ's gospel. I profess these with great consistency, but their impact on my life is not nearly so pervasive as it should be. The fact that I know the way I should travel better than many of my fellow human beings know their way merely adds to the shame of my persistent wandering from the direct course that Christ has plotted for me.

A fellow human traveler has been over the road. Even now as I try to maintain the course, He is beside me to call attention to the detour signs and keep me from driving off the highway.

Saving on Fuel Costs

To close the chapter, here are some hints for getting more mileage from your gasoline dollar. Most of them you have probably heard or seen before, but use these items as a checklist to be sure you are really applying what you know.

1. Driving at a lower speed gives you more miles per gallon.
2. Avoid rapid acceleration. Jackrabbit starts and sudden stops can increase your gasoline bills as much as twenty-five percent.
3. On crowded expressways, try to maintain a uniform speed and let your car slow down easily.
4. Keep your engine well-tuned.
5. Keep your tires properly inflated.
6. Never sit with engine idling for more than three minutes.
7. Instead of completely warming up the engine while standing still, drive slowly for a mile or so.
8. Change the oil regularly.
9. Drive without air conditioning whenever practical.
10. Plan where you're going before you start.

11. Park in a central location and avoid frequent stops and starts.
12. Avoid heavy traffic. The constant stop and go of crowded city streets burns up gasoline very rapidly.
13. Unload your trunk. Hauling excess baggage puts an added burden on the engine. All you need is a spare tire and a few basic tools.
14. Don't overfill your gas tank. A completely full tank will result in waste through spilling. It also adds to the weight of your car and decreases mileage.
15. Try car pooling to work, school, and related activities.
16. Talk yourself into walking or riding a bike to places reasonably close to home.
17. Let your kids arrange their own transportation sometimes. Having them check with friends for rides will lead to more sharing and saving.

10

What You Pay for a Swimming Pool Depends on How Far You Want to Get in Over Your Head

If you want a really splashy status symbol, you can't beat a swimming pool. Telling your friends about it will give you a warm feeling of success. You can put special stress on the words *"in-ground"* and describe the dimensions of the pool in round numbers (rounded *up*, of course).

Particularly impressive is a pool built in a unique shape. Country music singer Webb Pierce had one shaped like a guitar. You might go for heart-shaped, but kidney-shaped is passé.

We are very conscious of status, aren't we? We take pride in brown skin that comes from Florida, Hawaii, or the Bahamas, but we look down on brown skin from Alabama. We work hard to buy a bigger house in which we can close off some of the rooms to conserve energy. To afford that second home and a second car, we're willing to consider a third mortgage and a third job. Swim? Who me? Never—I'm too busy!

Contrast Christ. In the cool shadows of late afternoon, Jesus sat talking with his friend Mary. He had known Mary for a couple of years, and had come to enjoy these discussions very much. Mary was a deep thinker with a creative mind, always reaching out to know and understand more. Her personality was an interesting contrast to that of her sister, Martha. Martha was a first-class homemaker, full of vibrant energy, which she spent in keeping the house clean, the clothes washed, and good meals on the table. Lazarus, too, who had introduced Jesus to his sisters, was of a different type—retiring, self-effacing, and gentle, but dedicated to duty.

Jesus stopped to see his friends whenever he came near Bethany. The town was only a few miles from Jerusalem, and dining and relaxing with them provided an opportunity for refreshing fellowship.

On this particular day, Mary's questions to Jesus were particularly insightful. Eyes focused sharply on the Master's face as she listened to His answers, she seemed completely oblivious to the noise of jugs, pots, and plates clattering in the kitchen as Martha hastened to prepare the meal. Suddenly Martha appeared in the doorway, hands dripping wet, face flushed. As the late afternoon breeze blew refreshingly across her face, she eyed her sister Mary, rapt in conversation with Christ. There was censure in her eyes. Why should she have to work so hard to get the meal ready while Mary sat idly in the cool shade?

One Requirement

Christ had good advice for Martha. ". . . 'Martha, Martha, you are anxious and upset about many things; one thing only is required. Mary has chosen the better portion and she shall not be deprived of it'" (Luke 10:41,42).

"One thing only"! Not a lot or a yacht, not a country home or a trip to Europe, not even a backyard swimming pool. And certainly not all the stress that goes with striving to get ahead. The Lord has told us very clearly what that one thing is. He has given us His "first and greatest" commandment— the commandment of love. Mary's choice of the better portion was a commitment to the simple love of Christ, which prompted her to learn all she could from and about Him. She had chosen to keep her life, her love, and her learning uncluttered.

How pathetically cluttered our lives sometimes become!

We get so engrossed in earning a living, achieving success, or satisfying our personal needs that we neglect the one thing required. What is the remedy for this problem? How can we neutralize the dominant influence of our temporal and material concerns?

Take a break.

To follow Christ's advice and example, we need to force ourselves out of our obsessive preoccupation with material things long enough to regain perspective. And we need to renew this perspective often by taking time out for wholesome recreation. God gave us the model for meeting our need for recreation when He created the universe. Genesis tells us He made the world in six days and rested on the seventh.

Tragically, in my own lifetime we have given over our seventh day to the concerns of the marketplace. So enshrined is the ideal of being industrious and productive that we scarcely allow any time for tranquility and rest. Even the time we give to recreational pursuits is often filled with tension and hurry. Time to spare makes us nervous, like a hyperactive child with the constant question, "What can I do next?"

"We long for immortality," someone has said, "but we don't know what to do with ourselves on a rainy Sunday afternoon." In our pleasure-bent society, too many of us are pleasure-broke. We search frantically for activities to add to our enjoyment of life. All too often, satiation makes very little of what we do truly enjoyable.

French philosopher Jacques Maritain predicted that our opulent society would rot from within. He saw the spiritual, intellectual, and emotional danger in our obsession with egocentric pleasures. We are fulfilling his prophecy now. Our life of abundance, generated and nourished by technological advances and our instant credit system, has created a condition in which pleasure is no longer fun. Excessive boredom is a common American plight. Our natural capacity for fun has been dulled by the abundance of gustatory, visual, and oral delights pervading our lives. We have failed to preserve the rhythm of desire, anticipation, fulfillment, and regeneration.

How can we deal with this overkill that has robbed us of innocent delight? First, we have to recognize what real fun is. As rational beings the highest enjoyment of which our nature is capable is far beyond the realm of the physical senses. In fact some of the greatest enjoyment life offers has little or no relation to the body. Nor is it related to money or prestige. "That thou mayest have pleasure in everything," says St. John of the Cross, "seek pleasure in nothing."

What, then, is fun? We approach real understanding when we appreciate the pleasure a dedicated surgeon derives from his work. Once in a Chicago hospital, part of the ceiling of the operating room caved in during the course of surgery. So intense was the surgeon's concentration that he had to ask afterwards what all the plaster was doing on the floor behind him. Immersed in his task, he lost his sense of self and time.

Real fun is much like that. Psychologists sometimes call this intense involvement "flow." We become totally absorbed in the experience we are enjoying, surrounded by a feeling of well-being and refreshment.

The Cost of Recreation

Most Americans spend too much money having fun. I have friends who feel they aren't having fun unless they're spending heavily. Actually, there is little or no correlation between the cost of recreation and the benefit derived. If you don't believe this, try describing $50 worth of fun.

Looking back on your most memorable good times, you will probably recall a number of enjoyable activities of little or no cost. By contrast, some of the most expensive recreation you have bought has probably been the least enjoyable. Just being aware of the dent these flings put into our budget often takes away much of the fun.

125

It's Easier for a Rich Man to Enter Heaven

Our country today offers most of us enough leisure time to participate in highly creative recreational activities, which in earlier times only the wealthy could enjoy. Members of the average American family today can buy books and stereo records. They can join writers' groups or take music lessons. Concert halls, theaters, and museums are available for all. The wealth of our nation enables a larger number of people to participate in rich cultural traditions than ever before.

But finding free fun can also be a very enjoyable activity. Some families have discovered this while launching a crash program to pay off debts. They find the low-cost recreational activities so enjoyable that they continue them long after their debts are paid. Slowing down frantic spending is one way to find more time for ourselves. Spouses get to know each other better and are able to give more attention to their children.

Family Night

Obviously, the younger you start family activities with your children, the better. There will never be a better time than today. Right now, then, designate one night of the week for family night. Reserve this night consistently and make exceptions for the family as a whole, or individual members, only when it is absolutely necessary. On this night, let the family decide the kind of recreation to be enjoyed together.

You might, for example, try a night given to jigsaw puzzles. Smaller children generally have a few puzzles they enjoy working again and again. Encourage them to get these out so all the family can do puzzles together. For the older members of the family, there are certainly enough difficult jigsaw puzzles to offer exciting challenges.

Or you might try an evening of letter writing. Gather the family around one or more tables with stationery and pens. Decide which friends of the family should be written to on a given night, and divide these up among family members. The letters don't have to be long. Usually a series of short notes will be more effective.

Our family has derived much fun—and learning—from word games. Let me briefly describe three of our favorites.

You've probably played the game called "Ghost." There are several versions. One of the most popular begins by having one player announce a letter, say *P*. The next player then adds a letter, maybe *A*. Each player, in turn, tries to add a letter that will not make a complete word. When a player accidentally finishes a word, he gets a *G*, and the second time an *H*. A letter from the word *Ghost* is added each time a player completes a word. The idea is to outwit the other players by forcing them to finish words. If challenged after adding a letter, a player must prove he's building a real word. If he's bluffing, he gets a letter.

Another popular game is "Alphabet." In this game, the first player chooses a category, like cities, vegetables, or flowers. He begins by naming one example of the category, starting with the letter *A*. In turn, the other players move through the alphabet, giving other examples from the same category. For example, the first player might say "Atlanta." The next player might say "Boston," and the next "Chicago." If a player cannot think of an example beginning with the letter that comes up on his turn, he is out. The next player must try to name a city for that letter. Sometimes it may be necessary to go through the alphabet a second or a third time using new examples. The game goes on until only the winner remains. That player selects a new category.

The "Five-Letter Word Game" has been our family's favorite. Each player needs a pencil and paper. At the top left of the paper, each player prints a five-letter word of his own selection. The object is to guess the other person's word before he guesses yours.

Let's assume the second player has the word *track*. The first player starts by saying some five-letter word, for example *brown*. Since only one letter of *brown* (*R*) appears in *track*, the second player replies, "One." No other information is given beyond reporting how many letters of the guessed word are in the word the player has written at the top of his paper. Players take turns, each trying to guess the other's word.

Players will need to keep careful records of each move and an alphabet to indicate the letters that have been eliminated and identified. These records provide a good basis for guessing the word the other player has listed.

Watching and Listening

In most American homes today, television and recordings provide a large percentage of the entertainment menu. Having two or three TV sets in the home is more the rule than the exception. A wide variety of stereo systems, radios, cassette and eight-track players is available to provide the kind of music family members enjoy, and everyone knows each family member enjoys a different kind.

A 1978 national survey showed that watching television, listening to the radio, and listening to music at home were among the top five leisure activities of both men and women. All three were reportedly engaged in more frequently than social activities, sports, or sex. There goes another myth!

One of the more foolish purchases I've made in my lifetime was a "stereo-theater." These combination TV-radio-phonograph units are sometimes called "entertainment centers." They tend to be more attractive than practical. What you pay for is a large, over-priced cabinet, a large-screen television, and a stereo unit that doesn't provide good music because the speakers are too close together. But the most serious limitation is that only one of the three media—TV, radio, or stereo—is available at any given time. Investing in separate units may cost a little more overall, but you'll be able to suit more diverse family needs.

Unfortunately, much of the "entertainment" that comes

into our homes isn't very entertaining. Television is a tube that you often can't squeeze anything good from. Displeased with the quality of TV fare on France's National Television Network, one man took his set to the Eiffel Tower and hurled it nearly a thousand feet to the ground.

As an experiment, you might try *planning* an evening of television and follow it with an *evaluation*. Discuss the programs on the TV schedule for the evening, and let the family select the ones to be viewed. Watch them together and afterwards talk about their strengths and weaknesses. Sometimes a simple checklist form will make the discussion flow more smoothly.

There are, of course, many other inexpensive forms of recreation any family can share. Numerous board games are enjoyable. Non-electronic games usually permit more players in the same game. A variety of more active kinds of at-home recreation are available, such as table tennis, pool, and darts. Or, in good weather, you might move outside for badminton or croquet.

Your most valuable asset in locating inexpensive recreation is your imagination. Look around at the activities and opportunities for fun offered by your community. At the public library, for example, you can get books that will provide many hours of enjoyment. Participate in free film showings and lectures and explore local parks and recreation departments, which schedule a broad range of activities including concerts, dramatics, and athletics. Colleges and universities also offer diversified programs.

Social Gatherings

Sometime back, Hilda and I were invited to a social gathering involving many of the political, educational, and social leaders of the Cincinnati community. It was not at all the kind of party we're accustomed to attending. The event was held in a downtown auditorium and featured a musical stage production. After this performance, there were some speeches and then the food was served. We filed on to a stage to get our refreshments and then went back to our auditorium seats and balanced the plate of food and cup of coffee on our laps, trying to continue social interaction while we ate.

You've been to parties that have an atmosphere similar to that one. The situation seems artificial from the beginning. People hide behind their social masks, and it's very difficult to really talk to them. There is Mr. Richman bragging about his new Mercedes and telling stories of his intimate relationship with his boss. There's Mrs. Gabbard using gossip to tear down anyone who's making an effort to improve self or community. There are Mr. and Mrs. Mannequin strolling around the room with forced smiles and exuberance, receiving compliments about their fashionable clothing and beautiful bodies. Over in the corner are the Milquetoasts, quietly telling anyone who will listen about their insignificance and humility.

So many people, intent on making themselves look good while they feel bad! Social gatherings are an important form of recreation, but something deep inside me says we're doing it all wrong.

Not long ago, a Somerset, Massachusetts, man paid $2000 for a wedding. The bride wore a white veil, and the groom wore a top hat and a bow tie. Not at all unusual, you say? Well, this particular wedding united the man's two Labrador Retrievers. About 150 people attended. No stray canines were admitted.

Seeking Prestige

One of our problems is assigning too great a value to prestige. The decisions we make about how to spend our money are motivated by our desire to appear wealthy or to show the world our enjoyment of luxury. We drive our Porsches and our BMWs imagining that we are making an impression on others. Lakoste shirts and Topsider shoes are part of our trying to appear right up-to-date with fashion. We talk casually about exotic vacations or weekend visits to New York to see the shows.

Nothing sets us back like keeping up a front. Most of us would be satisfied with enough if the guy next door didn't have more. One reason living is so high now is that yesterday's luxuries always become today's necessities. Too many of us buy things we don't want, at prices we can't pay, on terms we can't meet, because of advertising we don't believe in the first place.

Our problem is not so much the love of possessions as the love of possessing. There is a difference. If we love our possessions and we are grateful for them, there is always the possibility of being lifted above the created object to love of the Creator. We can grow in love of God through the experience of loving His creations.

If what we love is not the possession itself but rather the act of possessing, then our love is subverted inside ourselves. We relish the power that comes with ownership. Compare, for example, two men who own original paintings by renowned artists. One displays his painting in a visible place and graciously accepts compliments. He is glad to be sharing the enjoyment of possession he cherishes. Sometimes he even takes time to contemplate the beauty of the painting when no one else is around. Not so with the man in love with possessing. His only joy comes from calling the masterpiece to the attention of his friends and watching their looks of envy. He is highly insulted if anyone does not recognize the masterpiece for what it is.

Life-styles

The standard of living for most Americans has progressed to the point where many of the expensive things we own are in twos or threes. We have two or three cars, two or three television sets, two or three telephones in the home. Some men I know even feel they're entitled to two or three women—and vice versa.

Around our house it's a bit different. We have two or three dripping faucets, two or three broken chairs, and two or three burned-out light bulbs I'll get around to replacing someday.

Simplicity should be an important value in our complex lives. The most godly men and women who ever lived, lived very simply. They did so not primarily because they were holier, but because they were smarter. Walking with God is simple; complexity is imperfection.

One of the major problems that comes with affluence is the danger of loss of this simplicity. Because we have many resources, we tend to get too intricately involved in them and fail to maintain a simple perspective. This is a very dangerous trap.

In his book *Peter's People* bestselling author Laurence Peter reports a growing movement toward "voluntary simplicity." He cites a 1977 study suggesting that 10 million American adults are currently living a deliberately simple life-style. Peter traces the roots of the movement and projects that it could encompass more than 90 million people by the year 2000. Many contemporary Christians are heeding Christ's call to more frugal living. Sometimes this response arises from conditions over which we have no control. Some of us have had jobs that seemed secure pulled out from under us. We have been forced to deal with the emotional turmoil and economic difficulties that go with such a loss. We may have had to accept a lower paying job or resign ourselves to the kind of living that can be provided through welfare or unemployment compensation.

Many others, though, are responding to Christ's call voluntarily. A few give nearly all of their possessions to a religious community or some charitable organization. Others merely seek everyday sacrifices through which they can share the advantages they have, thereby reducing their standard of living in accordance with the word of our Lord.

Many young, newly married couples find that the necessity of living on limited financial resources has a powerful unifying effect. The common goal of economizing to achieve some specific financial objectives draws them more closely together. They plan together, they save, and they look forward to the day when they will have more abundant means. But then when their financial condition improves and the pressure is off, they don't find the kind of relief they had anticipated. Instead, there's a feeling of sadness—almost regret. A common motivation that has brought them together has been lost. They realize that the difficult times had a vividness that intensified the experience of living and gave it added meaning.

How well I remember the early days of our marriage! I was a soldier, and we had an apartment fourteen miles off the Fort Knox military base. Our income was limited to the pay of a noncommissioned officer, plus the usual military allowance for quarters and for my spouse. Our first child was on the way, and we were eager to save enough money to make a down payment on our home when I was discharged.

Out of necessity we bought a second-hand car, but we did without a TV, phonograph, and a telephone. We ate economically and enjoyed very cheap fun. Those days of loving sacrifice provided the solid foundation for our life together.

11

The Bigger the Summer Vacation, the Harder the Fall

It's the end of a bright spring day, and I stand beside a lake watching the sun set. The spirit of blazing abandon that radiated across the morning sky is gone now. Subdued, the sun melts softly between the black branches of the trees. Ever so gracefully it makes its exit, drawing its reflection after it across the water.

From deep inside me comes a sudden urge to run after the disappearing sun. I want to follow its glistening path, escape the encompassing dusk, be absorbed in radiance.

What is the powerful yearning that sometimes grips our hearts at a time like this? It's a haunting blend of sadness and joy. It's a feeling of being carried. It's an awareness that we really belong somewhere else.

The yearning seems to come from down inside, like a pent-up force trying to get out. Our longing is to be part of the beauty we see, to identify with it, to become totally absorbed in it.

What attracts us at these precious moments is the reflection of the infinite beauty of God. Created to rest only in Him, our hearts are constantly disposed to yearning. If we have not hardened them by deliberately and repeatedly turning them away from their only true fulfillment, they will be naturally inclined to respond to God's attraction as metal to a magnet.

Most of us don't like being where we are. Wherever we are, we feel drawn to somewhere else. Perhaps if we run over just the next hill we can answer the appealing call of the promise of happiness. The monotony and drudgery of our lives seems to be the one thing hindering us from escaping into a larger and better world.

Recognizing the spiritual essence of this desire frees us to "bloom where we are planted." We know that as long as we are on this earth, our happiness will be incomplete. There is no place here that can satisfy all our wants.

Wherever we are, though, we can learn to like the place we are in. Even the dingiest dungeon can become tolerable; even inmates of concentration camps have found some pleasantness in their surroundings.

A sensible way to look at our present condition is, "This is where I am. I'll try to appreciate the good things about my surroundings." In this frame of mind, the street we live on, the house we reside in, the party we are attending become acceptable. Human appeal blooms in our neighbors, beauty in our backyard, and something interesting in the conversation of everyone who passes.

Here is the only place we can act. Even as we go through the routines of everyday living, we are fashioning for ourselves an eternity of uninterrupted joy. The adventure of eternity is prepared by letting God strip away those things that would keep us from perfect union with Him.

Getting Away

Appreciating our present surroundings doesn't diminish the value of getting away sometimes. We need vacations. To the value of changing the pace of *time*, vacations add benefits that come from changing our *place*.

Generally, those of us blessed with an appreciation of our current circumstances in life will also get the most benefit from a vacation. The magazine *Psychology Today* conducted a survey in 1980 to find out what kind of vacations people preferred. Over 10,000 readers responded. Most of the respondents who greatly enjoyed their vacations were the same persons who enjoyed their work a great deal. The survey yielded some other interesting findings: Men enjoy vacations less than women and also have a stronger sense of deserving more time off than women feel they deserve. Women consider work more important than men do. Men, though, are more eager to return to work after vacations, perhaps because they enjoy themselves less.

Most people fulfill their ambition to escape by going away at least once a year. The most popular vacation spots tend to be local beaches, parks, and forests. Only eleven percent of the respondents said they were content to stay at home and putter around the house during vacation.

Preparing for Vacation

Ah, yes, vacation! The time of exchanging good dollars for bad quarters. These days you can hardly get away from it all without meeting people who want to get it all away from you. You go away for a change and a rest, but the bellboys get the change and the hotel gets the rest.

If you are trying to figure how much you get for your vacation dollars, don't consider the number of miles you travel or the number of places you visit, but rather some index of how much real fun you have. Vacation should be a time of respite from the ordinary routine of our lives. After an opportunity to change pace, to have new experiences, and to refresh our minds and bodies, we can return to our daily duties more ready to invest ourselves wholeheartedly. A vacation that is not fun does not deserve to be called a vacation.

How can we best ensure that what we do with our vacation time is, indeed, fun? Simply stated, it takes planning. Possible alternative experiences must be considered and evaluated on the fun criterion. This is usually fairly spontaneous. If we don't feel like a certain kind of vacation, this is a good sign that it's not likely to be very much fun.

Sometimes we are wrong, of course. We base our preliminary evaluation on limited facts and impressions. We judge the attractiveness of a given experience without having enough information. More often, though, we accept certain kinds of vacation activities without even considering alternatives. We go where we've always gone, or for some other reason no other option occurs to us. Time spent in brainstorming or researching new possibilities is frequently beneficial.

Other forms of preparation can also be important to a truly enjoyable vacation. In general, the longer the vacation and the more people involved, the greater the need for planning time. One summer our entire ten-member family packed up and took off for Virginia Beach. Imagine our consternation when we discovered that no one had remembered to bring swimwear!

Psychological preparation is also crucial. With the right attitude, you can turn even the worst vacation experiences into worthwhile recreation. Finding yourself waiting in a long line to get into an attraction, for example, you can use the time to talk to others in the line and perhaps make a new friend. If rain interferes with your plans, you can explore museums or shops instead of sitting around and sulking. Getting yourself psychologically ready to have a good time is really far more important than packing the right clothes. The boys swam in their shorts at Virginia Beach, and Hilda got a new swimsuit out of the deal.

It is also important that you make some kind of budget for vacation. The form of this plan must suit your personality and needs, but in the beginning a fairly comprehensive budget is desirable. Estimations for each element of the trip should include how much you figure to spend on transportation, lodging, food, recreation, supplies, and miscellaneous.

When you have these expenses listed, dividing the total amount by the total number of days you plan to spend on vacation will give you a round figure that can serve as a general guide. If, for example, you allow $100 a day for everything except transportation, you will be able to judge whether your money will stretch over your vacation period by comparing your actual expenditures to this guideline.

Vacation and the Family

I believe it makes good sense to think of the variety of needs different family members have as we plan our vacations. Almost certainly, there is no single group of activities that can serve every person's interests. Through careful planning, though, we can distribute the time available so that each family member will derive considerable benefit.

One good strategy is to divide the available time into three segments. One part of the time can be given to recreation for the entire family. A second can serve individual needs by letting family members pursue their own preferences. A third portion of vacation time should be given to some form of service to others.

First, let's consider the family vacation. Such time offers one of the best opportunities we have to get to know one another better and reinforce the bonds of mutual love. Somebody said there are two kinds of travel in America: first class and with children. I guess it depends on how you get your kicks, but I believe traveling with kids is the highest class possible. They add such excitement!

To keep the kids quiet and out of trouble, a Martinez, California, man used to tell his, "Be quiet now and look for a sack of money." One day as they were passing through Dallas, Texas, one of the youngsters yelled, "There's a sack of money, Dad." The father pulled over and retrieved the sack. It contained $114,000 in checks, lost by the messenger service of the local bank.

Your efforts to promote family sharing at vacation time probably won't yield financial gain, but it's sure to have other value. Anyone who believes in the importance of the family can see an urgent need to find ways of solidifying it. Having fun together is one of the best means of strengthening family ties.

Your Personal Interests

Despite the importance of a family's sharing in vacation activities, most of us also have a need for pursuing our own unique interests. At the very least, most parents need to take some vacation time away from the children.

Hilda and I have made frequent use of weekends to get to know each other better. Short Saturday-Sunday trips offer an opportunity for parents—together or separately—to engage in activities of personal interest.

Special weekends are fast becoming a part of the American way of life. If our gasoline supply holds out, they may virtually replace the extended vacation to which many of us have become accustomed. One of the most important advantages of this form of recreation is variety. Sometimes, too, a husband and wife need to get away from each other: "I regret that I have but one wife to send to the country."

Some people turn to weekend recreational pursuits in remote places, such as the businessman who spends hours wading with his two sons in icy streams panning for gold. Others pursue avocational activities, often of a very active form. One doctor in the West, for example, gets his action as a weekend rodeo star.

Another challenging and rewarding kind of weekend can be found in the "weekend colleges" that are springing up all around the country. Their programs include a wide range of subject matter from art and photography to religion, geology, and foreign languages. By offering these, colleges are not only increasing their income, but are also providing stimulating and relaxing weekends for thousands.

Much of the fun and satisfaction of weekend recreation comes before and after. Planning, discussing, and keeping records can be a very enjoyable experience. The best approach is usually to make an annual plan around a number of major three- and four-day weekends. You don't have to schedule every such Saturday and Sunday, but you can line up most of them so that the essential arrangements are made well in advance. Such planning can also provide flexibility. You might want to work out a number of alternatives so that if weather or lack of finances forces a change in plans, you'll have some other activity to fall back on.

Others' Needs

Giving vacation time to reinforcing family solidarity and pursuing our own interests is good. Our vacation planning should also consider the needs of others. Parents should plan some of the vacation strictly around the tastes and interests of the children. Their minds won't be stimulated much on roller coasters and miniature golf courses, but they'll have fun. Come on, admit it. You're afraid of the Asteroid ride, and you can't bear the thought of another Putt-Putt defeat.

What can compare with the expressions of awe on children's faces facing the wonder of a gigantic souvenir shop or the deluxe swings and slides at the park? They stand looking over the splendor of the Grand Canyon, gaze at you with dreamy eyes, and ask, "How long will it be until the next ice cream store?"

Opportunities can also be found to give our time to persons outside our family. Entertaining shut-ins, sharing with the lonely, visiting relatives—these and many other forms of giving can bring us pleasure and renewal.

Leaving Your Job Behind

To make your vacation pay off, allow yourself some freedom. Many of us who are intensely involved in our jobs find it extremely difficult to leave them behind. We know if we take three weeks off work, we'll have to spend three months putting them back. The business man or woman who feels compelled to call the office occasionally just to make sure things are going well will have a hard time thinking only about sand and sea. A similar workaholic is the homemaker who finds unreal excuses for taking the kids along. Even if she does force herself to leave them behind, they go with her in her mind and cause feelings of anxiety for their welfare.

It is a mistake for us to think of vacations as a reward for hard work. Vacations have nothing to do with what we deserve. They are a matter of what we need. Thinking "I've earned the right to time off" results in a feeling of having to enjoy the vacation—or else.

Another frequent problem is that we wait too long to take time off. Exhaustion is a time for sleep, not a vacation. Being in good physical and emotional condition at vacation time is as important as it is at work time.

Finally, try to keep your expectations about vacation as realistic as possible. No matter how good the fringe benefit package your employer gives, it won't include a trip to heaven. Your vacation won't change you substantially; you won't come back a new person with all your problems solved. On the other hand, most vacations don't fall as short of the expectations we have for them as did that of a British couple who traveled to Wales for their summer holidays in 1971. Early in the week they joined a mystery tour. Unfortunately, the tour took them right back to their hometown.

We've had some that have come close, though. Once we were looking for an opportunity to take a short, inexpensive vacation with our children. A newspaper ad beckoned us to a midwestern city that shall remain nameless: "Take the kids to Urbia." The room rates were presented in an attractive package too good to pass up.

We soon found out why. It was a very old hotel. We could tell that from the outside, but somehow they must have built the rooms a half-century before the outside of the building.

The particular suite we were assigned had obviously not

been inhabited for some time—or cleaned. We reminded ourselves of how much we were saving, inspected the room carefully for vermin, and decided to make do.

When we were ready to wash up for the night, we discovered there were no towels. Well, we'd call for some. "We'll send them right up," we were assured. Several hours and phone calls later we gave up and went to bed dirty. Just as we were settling in for the night, a laundry worker, obviously angry at having been disturbed in the middle of her rest cycle, presented us with a handful of tattered towels.

Hotel Costs

Most of us who do any traveling have had similarly unpleasant experiences. Maybe you arrive at the hotel completely exhausted. The jet you were on negotiated the first thousand miles with ease, but that last two and a half of freeway travel did you in. You're happy to have a bed at any price. Somehow the desk clerk seems to know this. To your room rate he adds a dollar for each epithet you hurled at the interstate roadhogs.

What can you do about it?

There's no use talking to the desk clerk. Ask for the manager. If he or she is not available, insist that your protest about the room rate be noted and that the manager contact you at a specific time.

How successful you'll be in getting an adjustment depends largely on what promise you had received and how. If all you have is a verbal agreement by phone, your case is weak. Nevertheless, you may be able to get the local tourist or consumer office to come to your assistance. Generally, though, unless you plan to be in one spot for a long time, what you gain isn't really worth the hassle. Your best bet, if you are dissatisfied, is to move out—which is exactly what we did when we took the kids to Urbia. As I look back, I can't help but think of the *Boston Transcript* headline misprint: "Hotel Burns. 200 Guests Escape Half Glad."

The Bigger the Summer Vacation

On the other hand, it is sometimes possible to save substantially on hotel and motel rooms just by asking, in advance, "Do you have lower rates at any particular time of the year?" or "Do you have weekend rates?"

Resort hotels especially have high and low volume times. They routinely make special offers to increase occupancy at a time when rooms otherwise stand vacant. Weekend rates are designed to attract people for mini-vacations at times when business-related occupancy is off. Weekend packages and other special offers should be studied with care. Not all of them are the delightful bargains they seem to be. Be especially wary of "Vacation now, pay later" plans.

Camping

The very best way to save on room costs, of course, is not to use one. Camp. You get to soak yourself in Bug-Kill cologne and zip yourself into a sleeping bag that is sure to have a jammed zipper when you try to wiggle out in the morning. One-quart saucepans become bathtubs, and of course there is the constant enjoyment of feeling grit in shoes, shirt, and underwear.

The fun of a family vacation can be increased—and costs decreased—by camping. Imagine a rainy day with ten people crowded into a camper designed for six. What could be classier?

Camping is good for young people, even if it is only in theory teaching them how tough our ancestors had to be to conquer new frontiers of our country. Usually the teaching is more on the order of what the conquest might have been like if the pioneers had done it one week a year, on six wheels, to the background sounds of TV and stereo. Still, fun abounds and everyone learns valuable lessons of surviving a closeness that limits everyone's need for privacy. A child encouraged to pick up firewood or get a bucket of water is learning lessons of mutual help and love essential for his later life.

For my part, I enjoy the open road but not the open

plumbing. We prefer trailer camping in developed areas. One year, early in our camping experience, we loaded all ten of us into our station wagon, hitched an overstuffed Nimrod to the back, and headed for California. Our children at that time ranged from infancy to pre-teen. We drove 10,000 miles in thirty days, camped in some of the most God-forsaken places you can imagine, and changed several hundred diapers en route. It was still fun.

That vacation was just the most adventurous of many camping vacations we have had with the children. We started this vacationing style several years before it gained the popularity it now enjoys. We began by renting a camper for a few short trips, and when we saw that the family adjusted well to this means of lodging, we invested in one of our own.

A new Nimrod cost us about $800 in 1968. It has saved us thousands of dollars and enabled us to visit many places we could not otherwise have gone. If we had been able to afford more luxurious travel, we might have enjoyed it less. Certainly there would have been less variety; each Holiday Inn looks pretty much like the next.

Camping has also brought us close to nature. Novice campers are often warned about the dangers of being attacked by bears, especially in national parks. No one expects to have to deal with lions.

One night in New York, we pulled into a campground and set up our trailer. It was an attractive place with electricity, hot water, and other conveniences. Just as we were settling down for the night, my wife said, "What was that?" I told her that I had heard nothing. "I heard lions roaring!" she said.

Lions in New York? What could I say except to tell her to turn over and go to sleep? She was adamant. When I did finally hear the noise, I thought of several other possible explanations for the sound.

She was right. The next day we discovered that we were camped next to an amusement park with a special attraction—a lion tamer.

The Bigger the Summer Vacation

Unfortunately, the family that travels together often unravels together. What has worked well for the Felixes might be disastrous for you.

It was one of those long vacations that the Barnes family had been planning for a long time. The third day of stationwagon travel had been particularly rough. Dad finally found a motel that had a room and everyone sank wearily into bed. In a few minutes, the silence was broken with a tearful complaint from six-year-old Lynn. "Mommy," she wailed, "let's just go back home and live happily ever after."

Travel Expense

Whatever your vacation style, travel expenditure will be an important part of your budget. In these days of energy shortage, each of us has a duty to conserve. Low-energy vacations are possible. In most parts of our country, attractive and worthwhile recreational settings exist fairly close to home. If you have good reason to select a place farther away, choosing a single destination rather than several might save energy *and* give you more time to enjoy the place you choose.

Evaluate transportation costs carefully before making decisions about how you will travel. With gasoline, meal, and motel costs as high as they are, it may make surprising sense to travel by air. The secret of saving on flying costs is flexibility. As you plan, think of ways you can change these plans to take advantage of discount plans and special rates. For example, you may be able to change *when* you fly. Many airlines offer reduced fares at night, in midweek, or in off seasons. Weekend and family rates might also sometimes be available. Perhaps you can buy your ticket well in advance of flight time. Most airlines offer major discounts if you pay for your ticket considerably before your flight is scheduled.

A third possibility is changing *how* you will fly. Discounts are often offered to persons who will accept the crowded quarters of charter flights or to those who will fly with others

145

on tours or vacation packages. You might also be able to save by getting on a "standby" list for seats not taken by passengers with confirmed reservations.

Perhaps you can save money by changing the length of time you will stay at your destination. Excursion fares, for example, are offered to persons who agree to stay for several weeks between flights.

A final possibility is changing your itinerary. Sometimes an airline will sell you a ticket that is virtually a pass to their entire route network. An around-the-world package is one of the best buys available.

Whether you fly or drive, consider taking a bicycle along. This is much easier than you might think if you travel by air. Generally a bicycle counts as one piece of luggage. If in excess of the quota, it will cost you about $12 to transport the bike. You'll have to rotate the handlebars ninety degrees and you may be required to remove the pedals, but these inconveniences are minor compared to what you'll save in traveling short distances at your vacation site.

Cycling as well as walking and hiking can be planned as the major activity of your vacation. There are organizations that offer such body building tours at reasonable costs. One of the best, offering about five hundred organized tours each year, is the Sierra Club, 530 Bush Street, San Francisco, CA 94108.

12

Santa's Midnight Ride
Is Never an Economy Flight

Sometime ago someone did a study to determine what face was most widely recognized by young people. When my son read the results of this study, he asked me to guess who was most recognizable. I started guessing celebrities and then turned to current rock stars. All my guesses were wrong.

The face most widely recognized by children of all ages is . . . Santa Claus, of course! Young people everywhere know him immediately when they see his picture. The bearded countenance is unmistakable. And that seemingly bottomless sack he carries makes him more popular with young children than Miss Piggy.

In a way, Santa Claus' popularity is somewhat surprising. Very few people, after all, really believe in him. Nearly everyone knows Santa doesn't really come down the chimney; he comes through a large hole in Mom and Dad's pocketbook. Did you ever consider the irony of giving Dad a wallet for Christmas?

But the magic of Santa lives on. In one form or another, Santa Claus is universally loved throughout the world. Although his legend has its origin in Christianity, he is popular even in places where Christ has few professed followers. In Japan, for example, only one percent of the population call themselves Christians; yet the spirit of Santa is dominant at Christmas time.

Christmas in Christian nations, sadly, shows more awareness of Santa than of Christ. Each year Christ's birthday celebration is marred by excessive commercialism. His presence is nearly obliterated in the stampede of shoppers, His gentle voice drowned out by the whirring wheels and honking horns of holiday traffic. Increasingly people begin their celebration of Christmas early and end it even before the calendar year has run out. Decorations begin to appear in November; Christmas music is in the air throughout the early weeks of December. Christmas Day itself is actually a day most people are glad to get over with. By New Year's few Christmas trees still stand.

There is a frightening parallel here to the way we live our lives. Christ's coming has little impact throughout the year, as shown by the way we approach Christmas. We fail to appreciate the wonder of God's goodness in appointing Himself Son of Man. Our celebration of His Nativity is as empty as the discarded tree whose needles we sweep up the next morning.

Christian Giving

What an opportunity we miss in allowing our Christmases to be stripped of meaning! This season should be a time for strengthening the bonds of charity that unite us to one another. The gifts we give should be cherished by giver and receiver as our means of participating in Christ's generosity to us.

"Give, and it shall be given to you," the Lord has told us. "Good measure pressed down, shaken together, running over, will they pour into the fold of your garment . . ." (Luke 6:38).

Dr. Harold E. Hyde, president of New Hampshire's Plymouth State College, once gave what is probably the shortest commencement address in history. To the graduating class, he simply set forth three ideals: "Know thyself—Socrates. Control yourself—Cicero. Give yourself—Christ."

Certainly we could not have asked for a better model than

Jesus himself. Imagine! Christ, for all eternity the Son of God, becomes a man like us, to experience our humanity and offer the gift of His human self to the Father in atonement for our ingratitude. We can attain only a very imperfect imitation of His giving by trying to be aware of Christ's presence in our fellow human beings and especially in our loved ones. In striving for generosity and selflessness, we learn to give without expecting return—even the return of gratitude.

But our giving will always have flaws; our motives will never be perfectly unselfish. When the person receiving our gift does not respond appreciatively, we will feel some hurt or resentment. "It's not that I don't appreciate your gift," one woman told her husband. "But do you have to fight inflation singlehandedly?"

It is important that we avoid trying to equate the gift of *things* with true charity. Christian charity demands not so much the giving of something as the giving of someone. As our charitable acts are purged of selfishness, they more truly represent the giving of ourselves.

It hardly makes sense to call a dog to come if the dog is tied up. Similarly, it hardly makes sense to say we are giving ourselves when, really, we are tied up by our possessions. Our goal is detachment if we are to free ourselves of the bonds of selfishness.

Tired of repeated appeals for money, a man complained to his minister, "This Christianity thing is just one continuous give, give, give!"

The pastor thought a minute and then replied, "I think that's one of the best definitions of Christianity I have ever heard."

Surprise Gifts

"What do you want for Christmas?"

This question has become more and more common in our family as the children have grown older. Somehow it's not as easy as it used to be to delight them with surprise gifts, even if those are the ones that call forth an extra spark of delight and gratitude in their response.

It is a little more thrilling, isn't it? Getting the exact gift you asked for may be all right sometimes, especially if the gift is an unusual one. But if all gifts come from your suggestions, it's too much like just being handed the money and going out and buying things for yourself. When someone anticipates a want or need and surprises us, the gift is more unique. Creativity has been invested in choosing what to buy, and we like the surprise.

A Memphis man opened his car trunk one day and discovered a dusty package inside. He had bought a brass wastebasket for his wife as a Christmas gift, but had forgotten to give it to her. Sheepishly he took the package home and presented it to his spouse. When she saw it, she burst into tears of joy. It was their wedding anniversary and she was afraid he had forgotten.

When I read about this incident, I was a little surprised that a wastebasket would be so warmly received. As I thought about it, though, I realized that surprise gifts, regardless of what they are, are the best of all.

God often surprises us with His gifts. We ask for many things we feel we need or would like to have, but He's too great a God to limit His generosity to our requests. He knows our wants and needs better than we do ourselves, and He can supply them all. But sometimes when we get one of God's surprise gifts, we refuse to take it. All that is in us tells us that this isn't really something we need at all: the loss of a loved one, the career setback, the thwarting of an important plan.

The Lord helps us move toward joyful and enthusiastic reception of all His gifts. To be able to say, "Just what I wanted!" or even "If I didn't need it, you wouldn't be giving it to me," is an ability we all need to try to acquire.

Human gifts aren't always so practical. In 1887 Queen

Santa's Midnight Ride

Victoria of England was presented with a music box that had been designed especially for her, though it proved to be an incongruous surprise gift. The instrument was actually a musical bustle that would start playing whenever the wearer sat down and the tune it played was the British national anthem, "God Save the Queen."

Family Giving

Although giving and receiving are important in every aspect of our lives, family living provides special opportunities to grow through these sharing processes. In a Spirit-led Christian family, the giving that celebrates Christmas, birthdays, and other special occasions is symbolic of the spirit of charity that pervades 365 days a year—and some years, 366! The bond of charity is more durable than our dependency on easy chairs or golf courses. It even survives the powerful assaults of sibling rivalry.

The use of family financial resources provides a prime opportunity for learning and practicing the kind of sharing that undergirds true charity. Family cooperation in financial planning and expenditure creates the freedom that comes with voluntarily giving ourselves without reservation and eagerly accepting responsibility for others. In binding ourselves we are made free. In giving we receive. In uniting our own personality with those of other family members, we find out who we really are.

Tragically, money worries build a devastating tension in many families. The early signs of too much financial pressure are frequent discord in the family, excessive concerns for individual needs, and defensiveness about spending. In time, family members may start concealing purchases they make, even lying about what they spend. Angry accusations are flung and money begins to drive a fixed wedge between husband and wife and among other family members.

Carelessness, indifference, and selfishness are imputed and tempers flare.

Money just isn't all that important. When we lack the things we want or believe we need, we lose our perspective. Only by backing off a little can we renew our trust that the Lord will provide.

All members of the family should place their trust in God as they work realistically to provide for family needs. Hard times can lead to divisiveness and tension, destroying family harmony and unity. Or hard times can bring a family close together as they cooperate in solving financial problems and attending to one another's needs.

Sacrifice will always be easier to accept if all family members understand that it's necessary for the good of all. Each member's ability to give of himself or herself is a magnet that brings the family unit together at times of difficulty. Love, loyalty, and respect for the human dignity of each person in the family are both the basis and the result of this kind of cooperative effort.

Sometimes we concentrate too much on the sacrifices we have to make as parents. We need to be less concerned with what we are giving up for our children, whether it be luxury and comfort, a promising career, or just the everyday peace and quiet that will return with astounding suddenness when our children have grown. Rather let us think of what we can give, not what we must give up. Children cost money; that's obvious. Still we know there's no better investment in light of the lasting values we subscribe to.

Just how expensive is it to bring a child into the world and see him through to adulthood? Government figures indicate that if the value of the American dollar remains unchanged, children born in 1980 will cost the average American parent between $30,000 and $60,000 by the time they reach eighteen. Broken down by category, parents spend:

$9,000 to $13,000 for housing

$9,000 to $13,400 for food
$4,000 to $8,500 for transportation
$2,000 to $5,000 for clothing
$1,500 to $3,000 for medical care
$400 to $850 for education
$2,500 to $6,500 for miscellaneous.

College is additional, of course.

Teaching About Money

An English truck driver was stretched out asleep at home, his mouth open. His year-old son happened to come by and found the open mouth just too much to resist. He took a half-crown, about the size of a half-dollar, and popped it into his father's mouth.

Swallowing the coin woke the man up. Discovering what had happened, he rushed to the hospital. After the coin had been removed, the man explained that his son had no toy bank. "But," he said with assurance, "it will be the first thing I buy him when I get home."

Parents should teach their children about money. We have a duty to help our offspring develop sensible Christian attitudes toward our legal tender. Too often our sons and daughters see and hear us fretting over problems of inflation and economic shortage. The message we impart is that money is one of the most important things in life.

Now really, you know that's not true. Whether your child learns to love is immeasurably more important than whether he learns to balance a budget. Giving him an appreciation of the beauty of God's world is imparting a far more valuable gift than passing on a sizable financial inheritance.

Teaching children not to overvalue money is one key responsibility. Another is teaching them to manage it. Most psychologists and child development specialists agree that allowances help in this direction, though parents often have difficulty determining what a sufficient allowance is. This depends, of course, on your financial situation and the skill and responsibility your child shows in handling money. In general, the best bet is to provide an allowance large enough to cover specified expenses such as lunch, milk, books, and snacks plus a small amount to save or to spend as the child pleases.

The Influence of Affluence

For many American youths, the affluence of our society has been an overpowering condition that neither they nor their parents could manage. Too many parents have allowed themselves to be caught up in the game of providing every material thing they possibly could for their children. They have soon found that no matter what they do, it isn't enough. The yen for the ten-speed bike is replaced by one for a trail bike, then a motorcycle or car. No matter what is provided, there is always something else desired.

Never before in the history of the world has there been a group of young people so inundated with material surplus. This condition of extreme affluence destroys young people's sense of proportion, breeds stark materialism, and leads to a manner of thinking that regards a high level of material goods as absolutely essential.

Now our standard of living has tapered off, though we still have much more luxury than we know how to use well. Still, our incessant compulsion to reach out for additional material resources is waning, which will benefit our children. Giving too much is one of the most damaging things a parent can do for a child. Overgiving robs children of all desire to achieve on their own. It even takes away the child's belief that he or she is able to achieve things independently.

Too much giving is likely to make children overly self-centered and emotionally isolated from others. They are likely to grow up with the belief that the world is all take and no give. Inadequate tolerance for frustration will prevent the child from maturing to the degree of independence necessary for successful living.

Times of recession make it easier for parents to avoid saturating their children with toys and other material objects. Most parents can tell a child the family can't afford to buy him everything he wants. When the young person sees parents scrambling just to keep a good meal on the table, this message is even easier to impart.

In better times, it is more difficult to refuse children's pleas for material objects. Considerably more courage is needed to be able to say "No, I won't buy you a robot to do your chores for you," than simply, "I'm sorry; we can't afford it." The truth is parents *can* afford to buy these expensive things, at least as the child sees it. If not enough cash money is available, there is always the magic credit card.

Then, when Billy up the street gets a coveted item, there is added pressure. Guilt feelings set in for Mom and Dad. They feel selfish because they have spent money on themselves rather than providing what the child wants.

Whatever the economic conditions, we need to understand that we are helping our children when we don't give them everything they ask for. Teaching them to do without things passes on a worthwhile heritage. The young person who has learned to get along without develops a greater appreciation for actual possessions. The habit of doing without makes us wealthy throughout our lives.

Stretching Our Gift Dollars

We can stretch the money we share with others or spend on gifts in many ways. Two especially useful guidelines are to seek worthy charities and to do your Christmas shopping early.

In general, it is a bad idea to support your local street beggar. Most panhandlers burden society and seriously damage themselves by working hard to avoid work. Not only that but most of the pans they handle are shaped like whiskey bottles. Street beggars need our charity, but we give it more effectively in prayer and kind deeds than in cash gifts.

It is also important that we try to avoid giving our money to unworthy organizations. Unless you are absolutely confident that the charity appealing for your money is reputable, check it out. Get the address of the main office and ask others about this particular organization before you give. Don't settle for a phone call to a number provided by the solicitor. Some phonies arrange ahead of time to have a person at the other end give you a glowing report about a nonexisting charity. One estimate suggests fake charities collect about a hundred million dollars a year from careless contributors. As with any other kind of expenditure, you owe it to yourself to investigate before you give your money away. Any worthwhile charity will welcome your concern.

The second major guideline of early Christmas shopping gives you more time and flexibility to look for bargains. Markups on many items that accompany the commercial rush of the holiday season are also avoided.

Here is a list of some of the items you might want to buy for Christmas and the months you are most likely to find bargains:

Toys
  February, late December
Women's clothes
  January, March, April, May, July, August, October
Men's clothes
  January, February, May, June, July, August,
    October, November
Children's clothes
  March, April, May, June, September, November
China and housewares
  February, March, May, June, August, September

Sheets and towels
  January, May, July, August
Small appliances
  January, May, June, November
Radios and televisions
  January, February, September, October, November
Gift wrap
  late December

The three phrases that best sum up the Christmas season are: "Peace on earth," "Good will to men," and "Batteries not included." At 11 o'clock on Christmas Eve you're battling the crowd for last minute sales or struggling through the directions on how to assemble a new bicycle. Your eyes are blurred with fatigue and your nerves wound tight. "Never again," you tell yourself. "No more do-it-yourself assembling. No more gift-giving for me!"

When you see the joy of faces, young and old, in the glow of the tree, though, it's worth it all.

Generosity

Paul encouraged the Corinthians to be generous in sharing what they had just as Christ did. After an appeal for kindness, he reminded them: "You are well acquainted with the favor shown you by our Lord Jesus Christ; how for your sake he made himself poor though he was rich, so that you might become rich by his poverty" (2 Cor. 8:9).

But just how generous should we be in giving our possessions to others? This question arises frequently among sincere Christians. Our financial responsibilities, the needs of our families, and the uncertainty of the future, make us wonder just how much the Lord wants us to give.

Here is Paul's advice: "The willingness to give should accord with one's means, not go beyond them. The relief of others ought not to impoverish you; there should be a certain equality. Your plenty at the present time should supply their need so that their surplus may one day supply your need, with equality as the result" (2 Cor. 8:12–14).

A safe rule is giving a little more than we feel we can spare. This is a simple act of trust that the Lord expects of us. Whenever we look about us and see that the money we have to spend on recreation and luxury compares favorably with that of others about us, we can be confident that we are giving away too little. The story our Lord told of the widow's mite should convince us that real sacrifice is an essential ingredient in our giving to charity.

Giving to others makes us richer. Giving love is like giving information: We are not deprived of what we share. The common fund of Christianity is our sharing love in the mystical body of Christ, a sharing that increases our spiritual powers rather than draining them. We grow ever richer in the bounty of Christ's redemption.

13

The Worst Thing About Higher Education Is That It Keeps Getting Higher and Higher

It was homecoming and Oswald T. Floodgate returned to his alma mater, where his son was a student. When Oswald discovered that his boy was taking the same economics course under the same professor he had twenty-five years earlier, he decided to pay a visit to the class.

The professor was giving a test. He greeted Oswald and showed him a copy of the questions. To his dismay, Oswald recognized the same test he had taken many years ago.

"That's right," the professor granted. "I keep asking the same questions, but as the years go on I ask for different answers."

Economists' answers for our nation's problems are indeed changing—more rapidly than ever. Among the areas where these changes affect today's family, the cost of education is one of the most strongly felt.

In the 1981–82 school year, God willing, the Felix family will again have four full-time college students. For the first time all four will be living on campus. I'm not sure what courses they'll be taking, but I know what course I'll be taking. It's called Poverty 101.

There aren't many things I'd rather spend money on. Education is an investment in the human person which can't be taken away or destroyed. With my parents' help, I had the benefit of a liberal arts education that included three graduate degrees. No financial inheritance could ever be as precious.

Just as I did, our children are carrying a substantial portion of the financial burden of their education. This increases their appreciation and sense of accomplishment. It also makes it possible for Mom and Dad to put some money aside for such incidentals as food and shelter.

Even with the children's help we'll have to continue being careful since college costs are skyrocketing. According to the National Center for Education Statistics, American colleges and universities boosted undergraduate tuition by a record twelve percent for the 1980–81 academic year.

Dispelling Myths

Rising college costs have helped to dispel two myths about higher education. One myth is that a college degree is essential to anyone who wants to live a happy, productive life. The other is that the best way to earn a college degree is to enroll immediately after high school and go straight through. Let's look at the two myths separately.

In the first place, there have always been numerous career opportunities for persons who, because of lack of financial resources, limited intelligence, or free choice, do not have the benefit of a college education. Today's technological society has changed the picture somewhat, but it has by no means eliminated such opportunities. Viewed in terms of salary, working hours, benefits, and even personal satisfaction, some non-degree positions surpass many for which a college education is required.

Is a college education worth the price? One would certainly think so in view of the millions and millions of students who have decided their life plans call for higher education. Actually, the matter should be an individual decision. It is true that the average college graduate earns more money in his or her lifetime than the average person who does not complete college. Averages, though, are deceptively simple. For any individual faced with a career choice, they are almost meaningless.

It is also true that the personal development possible through a solid educational background can lead to a happier life. Education expands our capacity to enjoy life and what it holds for us. We become more sensitive to people, their cultures, and their art. Government, domestic and foreign affairs, and our rights and privileges as citizens are areas we study and debate in college.

There are, however, other ways to get a good education than by going to school—exposure to people, certain jobs, special interests, avocations, reading. Some ways, given enough motivation and self-discipline, are more efficient than others. For each of us there is a path of personal development which is most suitable, a path from which public opinion should not lead us astray.

The single most important consideration is a sincere desire to find that state of life that best suits our talents and interests as we perceive them. We can make the most of our intellectual capacities in many different ways. To believe that a degree and a professional career are indispensable places limitations on our search for God's will that can be a serious handicap.

Different Roads

Walnut Hills, Cincinnati's "college-preparatory alternative" school, has a deeply rooted academic tradition. Once, while I was a member of the school system's research and development council, we were discussing the school's requirement that junior high students take Latin.

One member commented that the requirement was outdated.

"Yes," agreed another council member. "People today have no use for Latin, *per se.*"

We kept the Latin requirement. I'm glad we did because I think a classical tradition has an important place in education. It's part of what our college preparatory alternative program stands for.

My key point, though, is that this kind of education isn't for everyone. In God's plan for our lives is an unlimited variety of patterns of service. Each of us is called to a unique life-style, in which we develop and use our personalities, characters, and talents in the way God has designed. Each of us must do what he or she is called to do.

Another essential factor is that, for any single dimension of human performance, not more than half of us can be above average. Sometimes too much emphasis is placed on high achievement and perfection. We have been trained throughout our lives to try to reach high standards. Teachers help us learn how to read, write, and compute. We make mistakes along the way, and yet there always seems to be someone who turns out a perfect paper. This perfection is set up as the goal for all to achieve.

Most of us would benefit in our education from some help in accepting imperfection. As long as the goal of perfection is held out as what is *expected* of us, we are doomed to failure. At the same time, few of us handle failure well, perceiving it as an attack on our basic personality.

In the early seventies a Somerville, Massachusetts, man named William Murphy graduated from Harvard at the age of 78. He took his first course at Harvard in 1927 and spent 46 years earning his bachelor's degree. As if that weren't enough persistence, Murphy indicated he planned to keep right on studying. His A.B., he pointed out, contained "only the first two letters in the alphabet. That's not enough for one man, even at my age."

Today more and more persons who are completing college are taking a more roundabout way to that goal. The traditional pattern was to enroll in a four-year college immediately after high school and, barring failure or some other misadventure, to march straight through. As the working world has become more complex and as college costs have accelerated, more students interrupt their education to work and save for a while. I see this as an extremely valuable opportunity for many young people. It gives them time to look around in the world of work and make their career choice on the basis of more information than they could ever get from textbooks or vocational guidance sessions.

Our Money's Worth

Whatever the student's goal and however he or she proceeds, we want to make sure we're getting our money's worth. For some young people "college-bred" means a four-year loaf made with Mom and Dad's dough.

A 1978 survey showed that getting a better job was the most common motivation for deciding to go to college, as expressed by three fourths of the responding college freshmen. Almost as many (seventy-four percent) decided to go to college to learn more. Sixty-eight percent indicated their motive was to get a general education, sixty percent to make more money, and fifty-seven percent to meet new and interesting people.

Before we spend money on education, we ought to be fairly clear about our motives. From a Christian view, the general aim of education is to train the whole man. To be complete, education must be directed at both the intellect and the will. Knowledge is in the intellect; character is in the will. Education, in other words, should both increase knowledge and build character.

Increase of knowledge is the discovery of God's truth. A well-educated person has the knowledge required to function effectively in his or her field of endeavor, but he or she sees this knowledge in the perspective of a broader background of truth about the universe. A basic concept of this perspective is the truth of our own existence. Would you buy an expensive gadget from a salesman without knowing what it was for? And yet some of us live many years without knowing why we are here or where we are going. The first knowledge education should provide is the answers to key questions like: *Who am I? Why was I created?* Acquiring extensive knowledge without clear answers to such questions is like trying to build a house in the middle of the ocean. A solid religious and philosophical foundation is the only means by which the crosscurrents of truth about the universe will make real sense.

Besides providing the factual knowledge we need, higher education should help us appreciate the relationship among the different fields of understanding. Too many colleges and universities today set out a broad range of courses for student choice without clearly recommending a structure integrating all the student learns. Courses ought to be arranged like a pyramid with some courses more advanced than others. The more complex subjects help to increase understanding in the lower-level courses. For example, the principles of metaphysics and logic shed light on mathematics. Mathematics, in turn, leads to comprehending physics and the science of the universe.

If a college education does not contribute to the student's philosophy of life, provide the factual and conceptual knowledge necessary to move forward toward life goals, and clarify the relationship among the various areas of knowledge, the student is not getting his money's worth.

Evaluating a College

It would be much easier to select a college if they came marked like eggs, meat, or canned peaches. When we chose Grade A Large, we'd know what we were paying for. Unfortunately, it's harder to judge how good a school is or collect all necessary data for making a decision. Studying college catalogs is one of the most valuable sources of necessary information. Accreditation, qualifications of staff, diversity of course offerings—all these essential characteristics can be partially evaluated through the catalog.

The second step is to talk to as many people as possible who know something about the colleges the student is considering. This includes counselors, admissions officers, teachers, alumni, and current students. Don't ignore the dropouts—they might have real insight into the problems the student will face at that particular school. And finally, what you hear and read about specific colleges and universities will help you evaluate them, but don't base your entire judgment on isolated pieces of information.

To give a more complete picture, most high school guidance departments now have commercially prepared "college search" programs. Some of these are computerized; others simply offer the student a rather easy means of identifying colleges with specific curricula or characteristics. These programs are a good way of narrowing the range to a few institutions that hold the most promise.

If at all possible, it's a good idea to visit at least two or three of the colleges under consideration. Being there gives a more reliable impression of the atmosphere of the institution, the adequacy of its facilities, and the interest staff members take in helping students. It's best to solicit the help of the admissions office in planning such a visit.

What It Costs

Twenty or so years ago, when those of us with children currently in college were starting to plan for financing this venture, $6000 would have covered the full four-year cost of most of the schools of our country. Today these costs have spiraled, with $30,000 not an unusual total. The cost of a college education has far outstripped the increase in disposable income.

Concurrently, the availability of scholarship funds has declined, especially for people within the middle-income range. Parents are now expected to put up far more money than we ever thought we'd have to as our contribution to the student's total costs. Most of the large sums of financial support go to the students from poor families and to athletes.

This is not to say that the middle-income parent's search

for financial support will inevitably be futile. It is usually possible, with enough effort, to come up with a financial package that will make the college of your offspring's choice affordable. In most instances, though, part-time work and loans will be a part of this package. Even the very capable student is not likely to receive more than a third of his or her college expenses as an outright grant.

The financial plight of the state of New York has been widely publicized in recent years. Not long ago, the state legislature required the city university to impose tuition on its students. Realizing that this would cause hardship for students of limited means, the university offered assistance through the financial aid office and advertised that students should contact the office at 999-1234, a number formerly assigned to Dial-A-Joke.

Being able to afford a college education today is mostly a matter of motivation. Determination on the part of the student and his family is necessary in seeking out accurate information and in avoiding decisions based on misconceptions or myths. Too many students with great promise let the price tag scare them away from certain colleges and universities. Even though it is very difficult for people of average means to get outright financial grants, there are many other forms of financial aid available to the determined applicant.

At some colleges as many as eighty percent of the enrolled students are getting some form of financial aid. In all, more than $12 billion is available to help students pay for education they could not get on their own. While actual costs vary considerably from one college to another, the share of the individual family in those costs is fairly uniform.

Where to Look for Help

The first sources of information to consult in seeking financial aid for college are the high school guidance counselor and the financial aid administrators at the colleges the student is considering. Many high schools have career and counseling centers in which there is abundant information about colleges, the courses they offer, and the expenses they entail. Personal contact with the counselor will save many hours of rummaging through these materials and also provide a supporter of the student's cause.

The director of financial aid at any college has as his responsibility knowing exactly what financial assistance the institution can provide. He is in the best position to give the student accurate and up-to-date information about available resources, both those provided by the college itself and the numerous complex sources from outside. Besides that, the financial aid director will be making—or strongly influencing—decisions about the merits of your case.

Federal, state, and college financial aid programs are the primary sources of help. In each program the key to obtaining financial aid is demonstrating a need. The student must have evidence of being unable to pay all the costs associated with college attendance.

There are three basic steps in estimating how likely it is that you will get financial aid:

1. Learn the costs at each of the colleges the student wants to attend. Include estimates of tuition and fees, room and board, books and supplies, transportation and personal expenses. Room and board costs should be estimated even if the student plans to live at home.
2. Estimate the amount the family might be asked to pay of those costs. Most often this amount depends on the results of an analysis performed by a national organization such as the College Scholarship Service. Completion of the Financial Aid Form provides the information necessary for this computation.
3. Determine the amount of financial aid you will need by subtracting your share from total costs.

It's Easier for a Rich Man to Enter Heaven

Loans for College

For families who have not been able to set aside money for college, borrowing may become necessary. Some families find it convenient to obtain second mortgages on their homes if interest rates are favorable at the time. If the family has a backlog of assets to offer as collateral, it may be possible to get a regular bank loan at current rates of interest. Other loans are often available as part of financial packages offered through the college financial aid office.

The 1980 Higher Education Act is making it easier, but more costly, for middle-class families to borrow money for college. To help students whose family income level is too high to quality for most grants, the law appreciably expands the amount of government-insured loan money available for middle-class students. At the same time, it raises the interest rate on these loans from seven percent to nine percent for new borrowers after January 1, 1981.

Under the Guaranteed Student Loan part of the law, an undergraduate may borrow up to $2,500 a year for five years. Students not dependent on their families may borrow up to $3,000 a year, and graduate students may borrow as much as $25,000.

For National Direct Student Loans the law raises the interest on the loan from three to four percent for new borrowers. The limits on these loans, based on financial need, range from $3,000 to $6,000 for undergraduates to $12,000 for graduate students.

Other means of financial aid addressed in the law are Basic Education Opportunity Grants for students with family incomes below $25,000 a year, supplemental grants for needy students, and work-study jobs.

Jobs for College

The old "working my way through college" approach still has much to recommend it. College-bound high school students frequently take summer and after-school jobs. These positions are somewhat scarce, but the upsurge of fast-food restaurants has increased the availability of employment for many older high school students. Others are able to gain employment requiring special skills such as typing, sales, or house painting.

With our children, I have planned to take care of about half the cost of their college education and to let them carry the responsibility for the rest. This has worked out well. Those of our offspring who have strong academic leanings find ways to meet expenses through part-time and summer employment and a very tight budget. Because they have less money to spend on recreation, they have more time to give to their books.

Several of our children have chosen to interrupt their college education to spend a half year or more in the working world. Besides putting money in their pockets to attend to future expenses, this has given them an opportunity to get a clearer sense of direction for their future careers.

The best way to obtain a college job if a student has no leads is to register at the college placement office as early as possible. Chances for placement will be appreciably increased if the student has a skill such as typing, bookkeeping, computer operation, or gardening. Generally, the student will not have to be academically above average to get a job. Nor will demonstrated financial need be required, although top priority is likely to go to the most needy students.

Many colleges have a cooperative work-study plan that enables the student to earn a substantial portion of his college expenses. Students in these programs generally work full-time for a portion of the year and attend school the rest of the year. In most situations, the college helps to locate jobs for students in fields closely related to their college majors.

Such co-op plans have much to recommend them. Besides monetary benefits, the student gains valuable work experience. He gets to apply the information he is learning in school, and his education is likely to have more meaning as a result. In addition, co-op students are often offered full-time positions with the companies for which they have worked during their school years.

Other Possibilities

If a student does not qualify for financial aid for college, there are still ways of cutting costs. Let me list just four:

1. Choose a college with lower costs. The least expensive alternatives are a public two-year college and a state college with the student living at home.
2. Investigate the special payment plans that some colleges are developing to help families that can't meet the costs.
3. Attempt to get credit by examination, thereby reducing the number of credits for which the student must pay.
4. Carry heavier course loads to compact the college degree requirements into less than four years.

If you start early enough, one very sensible approach to preparing to meet college costs is setting up a temporary trust with the young person as income beneficiary. This requires some advance planning as well as capital, but if your children are young enough such a procedure will help you deal with whatever situations an inflationary future may hold in store.

What you do is set up a short-term trust for the child for a minimum of ten years. Invest enough in securities or other properties to pay the child a reasonable annual sum, say $2000 a year. This income is tax-free for the young person, and you will get back the income-producing property when the trust ends. With the income that is produced split away from your own, you may find yourself in a lower tax bracket, thereby saving even more.

It's obvious, I think, that paying for college is no easy matter for most of us. It helps if you start saving early. Whatever money parents put into the education of their children is likely to be a good investment. As I have tried to make clear, though, the best returns usually come from ensuring that educational choices and decisions fit the individual student and from involving the student in paying for college.

14

I Recently Bought a Retirement Policy; If I Keep Up the Payments for Twenty Years, My Agent Can Retire

If you're willing to pay for it, you can get insurance on anything—well, almost anything. You can buy protection against floods, earthquakes, and special risks. You can get credit insurance to handle your bills if you are disabled or deceased. You can buy vacation insurance, boat insurance, pet insurance, and insurance on various parts of the body.

Now there is talk of divorce insurance. I haven't seen it advertised yet, but I read of a New York attorney who is convinced that companies should begin to issue divorce insurance policies. Patterned after automobile insurance, the policies would be designed to provide necessary financial support to ease the monetary problems of a recently divorced couple. The attorney goes so far as to suggest that with the soaring divorce rates of today, such a policy might make a very sensible wedding gift!

Limited Coverage

It has been said that buying insurance is much like wearing a hospital gown. Your coverage is never as much as you think. There are some kinds of protection we would like to have that no commercial insurance policy can provide.

Years ago an American life insurance company opened a branch in Shanghai, China. Even before the company started advertising its services, the office was jammed daily with Chinese men demanding policies.

I Recently Bought a Retirement Policy

A few weeks later the manager found out why. One of the residents who had taken out a policy passed away. Other policy holders organized a mob and wrecked the office. They were convinced that the insurance manager was a fraud because the man's life insurance hadn't kept him from death.

And what about eternal life? For most of us, the assurance Christ has given that we will spend our eternity with Him hinges on our wholehearted acceptance of His salvation as reflected in the actions and decisions of our everyday lives. The complexity of daily living interferes with the sense of security we'd like to have about our eternal destiny.

Christ's death on Calvary was the one-payment premium for God's insurance policy on our eternal life. Taking upon Himself the full burden of our guilt, Christ provided a payment for sin as only He could do. As a result of this wondrous sacrifice, we are assured an endowment that will bring us the endless fulfillment of all our needs.

But we have to accept it. Christ has banked a trust fund for us beyond the reach of rust, moths, and thieves. We are free to decline, though, and choose instead the continuous and unending frustration of never having our need for Him satisfied.

There is a parallel here between our assurance of eternal life and our insurance of earthly lives and possessions. Just as the many contingencies of our complex world keep us from being totally secure about our salvation, so also these same complexities cause considerable confusion about the insurance policies we keep in our personal files. Most of us could not say offhand how much health insurance, life insurance, or auto insurance coverage we have. We're even less likely to be aware of the limits of what the insurance will pay or the conditions for payment spelled out in the fine print.

Legal language must be complex to cover the almost unlimited possible circumstances that arise with insurance claims. With language that must stand up technically in a court of law, insurance policies almost inevitably are difficult to read and understand.

Unfortunately, nothing makes small print more legible than an accident. The story is told of a man who filed a claim that his car had been demolished in a wreck. When the insurance adjuster contacted him, the man patiently answered the adjuster's questions and then asked how soon he would get his money. Politely but firmly, the insurance representative explained, "Our company's policy is not to give you money. We replace the car with a new one."

"If that's the way you do business," the man said indignantly, "you can cancel the policy on my wife."

Selecting Your Agent

Obviously, it's important to do business with a reputable insurance company. Of the 2000 insurance companies in the U.S. and Canada, probably only about 800 are truly reputable. Reasonable care in selecting a company you can depend upon involves examining the company's financial record and being sure it is licensed in your state. Try to learn something about the customer-service orientation of the company, especially its track record in paying claims.

After all, you don't want to try to collect on your group insurance and find out that the entire group has to be sick at the same time. "When I took out the auto insurance policy," one young woman complained, "I didn't realize that it was $100 debatable."

Any questions you might have about a company or an agent can be referred to the insurance board in your state. It's worth taking the time and effort necessary to get the answers you need. Bad insurance advice can cost you a lot of money. Even more seriously, it could cost your family a great deal of grief if you should die.

Choosing an insurance agent demands the same kind of care you would take in selecting a lawyer. If the agent does not come recommended by friends you can trust, ask him or her to provide references. A helpful, knowledgeable insurance agent is one of the best friends you can have. There are plenty of good agents out there, but there's no easy way to find one. If you look in the Yellow Pages under "Good Guys," you'll find that letting your fingers do the walking is not particularly helpful in this case.

The kind of agent you want is one who is interested enough in your welfare to give you good advice. He has to know his business, but he also has to know your personal needs well enough to recommend the best coverage to fit those needs. Above all, he must be ethical. You don't want him selling you insurance you don't need or policies that are not entirely appropriate to your situation.

Your best bet will usually be a general agent, one who can sell you policies from different companies—policies to cover your life, your house, your car, your other possessions. Such an agent can selectively provide you with the ideal coverage. He can fight for you when necessary. He will be available to answer your questions as they occur.

Be wary of an agent who urges you to change companies or switch policies. Before you make a change, study the situation thoroughly. If you decide that a change is in order, try to move in the direction of consolidating your coverage with a single agent.

Feeling completely comfortable with your agent is a product of your confidence that you can trust him to seek your best interests. If you have such an agent, take good care of him. Give him all your business, and tell your friends. The turnover among insurance agents is high, and you want to make sure your "good guy" is around for a while.

Life Insurance

Our family life insurance agent is an affable gentleman, eager to be of service and careful to avoid high-pressure techniques. Like many other insurance agents, ours makes a point to send each member of the family a birthday greeting every year. This is a gesture we appreciate, although we frequently joke about it. Our agent has just two types of birthday cards, one for male clients and one for female. He must have bought 10,000 of each. I figure that in the fifteen years or so that he has served us, the Felix family alone has received over one hundred of the masculine cards.

There's a touch of irony in receiving a birthday greeting from an insurance man. It's as if the life insurance company were saying, "Congratulations, we won again this year! Better luck next time."

Insurance companies aren't really gamblers, of course. The structure of their benefits and premiums is designed to insure profits. That's how it should be. An important part of the security provided by insurance is knowing that the company will have adequate resources to pay the benefits when they are needed.

Life insurance benefits are important for our survivors. The high cost of death today suggests that we make sure those who survive us have money enough to dispose of our mortal remains. In addition, if others are dependent upon us, we want to make the best provision we can for meeting their needs after we are gone.

It remains true that not everyone needs life insurance. If you are single, divorced without children, or married to a self-supporting spouse, there may be no good reason for you to have life insurance. That doesn't mean agents won't try to sell you policies. They'll argue that you can save money by buying your insurance at an earlier age. You should know that this is true only because you will be paying over a longer time. You are not receiving the benefits at a lower overall price by starting your payments earlier. In the same way, the argument that you might be uninsurable sometime in the future is a weak one because the odds are so much against this possibility.

Assuming you do need life insurance, how much coverage should you buy? It's poor economy to take out so much insurance that you have to starve to pay the premium. Unfortunately, there is no good way to determine how much life insurance any of us really needs. None of us knows when we will die or what our economic condition will be at that time. You simply make educated guesses. At best, try to provide sufficient insurance coverage to take care of survivors if you were to die in the immediate future.

One approach is to sit down and draw up two columns, one for liabilities and one for assets. Consider first what your survivors would have from your estate, from social security benefits, and from their own earning power. Compare this with the expenses they would have to meet based upon your current operating budget. Add the cost of a funeral and some provision for illness or injury. Your life insurance coverage should at least take care of the difference between the liabilities you compute and the assets you can project.

Types of Life Insurance

Two major types of life insurance exist, term and cash value. Term insurance, as the name implies, provides coverage only for a specific number of years, although it may be renewable. A cash value policy, on the other hand, provides protection as long as the insured lives and maintains the premium payments.

Most often, insurance companies and their agents will promote cash value policies as the basis of all life insurance programs. Many insurance experts, however, believe that term insurance is more appropriate for most persons. Both types of coverage have advantages that you should know enough about to select the package of coverage that's best for you. Often this best package includes a combination of both cash value and term insurance.

Cash value policies come in several different forms, the most common of which are straight life, endowment, and variable life. Straight life is the most popular form; it includes two elements—a life insurance protection element and a savings element. Endowment coverage is similar to straight life except that it matures after a specified number of years, with the face amount of the policy then paid to the insured. Variable life policies provide that a portion of the premiums be placed in a fund from which stock purchases are made.

The cash value of an insurance policy is in many ways like a savings account with some key differences. Money in a savings account can be withdrawn at any time at no cost. To get the cash value of an insurance policy, on the other hand, you either have to give up the policy or borrow from the insurance company with your cash value as collateral. If you choose to borrow, interest must be paid to the company. In other words, the cash value of an insurance policy is less accessible than money in the usual savings account.

There is another angle to be considered, though, especially if you happen to be in a relatively high tax bracket. The interest paid to you from a savings account is taxable with every year's declaration. The buildup of cash in insurance policies, on the other hand, is not taxed until you surrender the policy. Even then, it is taxed lightly.

Term insurance offers pure protection with no savings element included in the policy. When the contracted term ends, a new contract must be entered into if the individual wishes to remain insured. The cost of this next policy will increase because growing older has increased the risk of death.

The major advantage of term insurance is that it is relatively inexpensive in the early years when most of us have more limited resources. In addition, the lower premiums allow the insured to put the money that is saved into investments that might yield higher returns than the cash value insurance policy.

Health Insurance

As with life policies, health insurance policies tell you everything you need to know about the extent and condition of coverage. Unfortunately, the terms are presented in complicated language, and often we are led to believe that the coverage is more complete than it really is. If you take time to read the policy carefully, you will find that the language precisely defines just what is and is not covered. If necessary, have your agent or some other knowledgeable person explain the terms of the contract to you.

Many of us obtain our health insurance as a fringe benefit linked to our jobs. How else could we afford it? Because we're not paying directly for our health insurance coverage, we are often not familiar with its provisions.

Medical care is very expensive. Coupled with the impact of inflation has been the expense of some very sophisticated medical technology and equipment, such as open-heart surgery and dialysis machines. Medical costs have skyrocketed. Tragic results have come to families in which long-term disability has been incurred. Loss of income, doctor's fees, hospital rooms—add these up and you have an equation for financial disaster. Total protection against such a situation is not possible. The most we can hope to do is cushion the impact through realistic medical and disability coverage.

A good package of health insurance includes coverage in five areas: hospital expense, doctors' bills, surgery costs, major medical expenses, and disability income. Typically, two or three policies are needed to provide this total range of coverage.

The key question with regard to hospital expense insurance is how many days of hospitalization are covered. Also, you'll want to know whether benefits begin with the first day of hospitalization. Read your policy carefully to see whether it pays the full hospital bill, some given percentage, or a fixed daily allowance. You can expect to pay more, of course, for policies that cover the full bill for a reasonable length of time. You'll have to judge whether the level of coverage meets your needs.

With insurance to cover doctors' expenses, figure out whether the policy covers treatments only in a hospital or in the doctor's office as well. Understand how much the policy pays for each visit and what limits there are on the number of visits.

Know whether your surgical insurance coverage provides benefits on a flat rate schedule or on a percentage of the actual cost. If your policy specifies a flat rate, compare the benefits with what surgeons are currently charging for the various types of operations. Also, familiarize yourself with the exclusions written into your policy and the amount of deductibility.

Deductibility and exclusions are also important with regard to your major medical coverage. The most important factor in this area, though, is the maximum amount of benefits the company will pay you. Remember that major medical expenses can quickly run into thousands of dollars. Know whether the maximum stated covers your entire lifetime or whether it can be restored again after you recover from a given illness.

One of the most important things to know about disability income coverage is the waiting period between the first day of disability and the starting time of the benefits. The longer the waiting period, the lower the premium will be. At the same time, though, you'll lose more money if you do become disabled. Acquaint yourself with how your policy defines disability. Be wary of a clause like "inability to perform duties pertaining to *any* occupation."

Be wary also of health insurance purchased by mail. Sometimes it's very difficult to determine exactly what coverage you are paying for. Many people have had the painful experience of discovering that their policies did not cover a specific illness or type of hospitalization expense.

I Recently Bought a Retirement Policy

What happens many times is that advertising copywriters develop attractive mail "communications" that communicate very little. The insurance underwriter may be completely legitimate but the limitations of coverage are hidden in fine print so that you think you are getting coverage that just isn't there. For example, health insurance policies universally specify a number of days of illness that must occur before benefits are received. If that period of time is a full month, it's somewhat unlikely that you will ever collect anything. Some policies also have a "coordination of benefits" clause so that they pay off only after other health insurance benefits have been exhausted.

The details of benefits and premiums are almost never completely understandable. Not long ago, the clergy of the Spokane, Washington, Roman Catholic diocese got into a hassle with Blue Cross. The diocese held a group medical policy on its sixty-six priests. Blue Cross had added thirty cents a month to the premium for each policy—for maternity benefits.

Automobile Insurance

The cost of automobile accident repairs has escalated beyond inflationary norms. With more and more automobiles on the highways and with modern expressway systems facilitating higher rates of speed, the money paid out in accident insurance claims has mounted almost beyond imagination. The result has been exorbitant auto insurance premiums that are prohibitive for many of us. The Felix family now includes seven drivers in the teens and early twenties. Coverage has been possible for us only because the young drivers share in the cost.

One result of these high rates is our eagerness to economize in any way we can. The best way to save money on auto insurance is to maintain a good driving record. Insurance companies do not take serious risks without passing the corresponding expenses along to policy holders. With a poor driving record, your premiums will be higher. Some companies will cancel your policy after a few costly accidents.

Sometimes, it is possible to obtain a discount if you have driven for a while without an accident. Other savings may be available to drivers of compact cars, to young people who have completed driver training courses, or to students with a good academic record.

Generally, the amount of your premium will be based on a number of factors, the most common being the following: your driving record; estimated annual mileage; use of car for business versus pleasure; make, model, and age of car; where you live.

Automobile insurance includes five basic types: liability, collision, comprehensive, medical payment, and uninsured motorist. Liability insurance covers personal injury and property damage to others for which you are held responsible. Collision insurance takes care of damage to your own car and will generally include some provision for the owner paying the first $100 or so. Comprehensive insurance provides coverage against fire, theft, vandalism, and other accidents stemming from natural causes. This will also generally include a deductible provision. Medical payment insurance covers hospital and medical costs incurred by you or your passengers in an automobile accident. Finally, uninsured motorist insurance covers injuries or damages caused by a hit-and-run driver or one whose insurance is inadequate.

The most common savings on these types of insurance come from maintaining relatively high deductible amounts and dropping the collision insurance as the car gets older. A $200 deductible clause has become almost standard. Even a minor accident can result in damage that exceeds this amount. You would probably want to pay smaller bills out of your own pocket anyway to keep the cost of your premium down. Obviously, as the value of your car depreciates, it makes less sense to maintain coverage on the vehicle itself.

You might also be able to save a considerable amount on your car insurance by comparing rates among companies. This is especially true if you have a good driving record. Different companies charge considerably different premiums for policies that provide similar protection. One reason is insurers compute premium costs in various ways. Companies also differ in the amount of money they spend on overhead costs such as advertising and commissions. Shop around and choose the reputable company that offers the best rates for the coverage you need.

Homeowner's Insurance

There is no place like home—no place so important to protect against loss through fire or other disaster. The possessions you keep in your home need to be insured against theft, and you need protection against liability for accidents that may occur on your property.

Inflation has jumped so fast that most of us haven't realized the changes called for in our insurance coverage. A house that would have cost $25,000 ten or fifteen years ago would now cost about $75,000 to replace. If you have not added to your homeowner's coverage with each renewal, you have probably not kept pace with inflation. The protection you're carrying should be equal to eighty percent of the replacement of your home, not including the land. Insurance companies will pay full replacement value only if you are at or above eighty percent coverage. Otherwise, payment will be made on a depreciated basis.

Let's see what this means. Say your ten-year-old living room furniture is destroyed by fire. At the eighty percent level or above, the company will pay what it costs to replace the furniture at today's prices. Below the eighty percent standard, the company might pay only half the replacement cost.

Affording the insurance coverage we need is sometimes a

real problem. As with auto insurance, one way to deal with the rapid increase in costs is to change the policy to include a higher deductible amount. Homeowner policies typically will carry a provision for $100 or $200 deductible. You can save money by going to a $500 amount or even to $1000 deductible. The general principle involved in such decisions is to protect yourself against big risks and let the smaller ones take care of themselves.

Perhaps you heard about the insurance adjuster who returned to the office after investigating a fire that had gutted a home.

"What was the cause of the fire?" his boss inquired.

"Friction," the investigator told him. "The fire was caused by rubbing a $100,000 insurance policy against a $60,000 house."

Wrap-up

To review, there are at least six ways you can save money on insurance without depriving yourself or your loved ones of adequate protection. It will take some effort and a clear willingness to work at making the best use of your financial resources.

1. Get yourself a trustworthy agent who represents one or more reputable companies.
2. Try to obtain as much of your total range of coverage as possible from this single agent.
3. Use your agent as necessary to help you understand the details of your various insurance policies.
4. Don't let your trust in your agent keep you from comparison shopping as you consider new types of coverage.
5. For coverage other than life insurance, consider possible savings through higher deductible amounts.
6. Know that even with the best insurance you can pro-

cure, it is foolish to insure a life on earth that is not enrolled in heaven. Invest the rest of your life by surrender and obedience to our Lord Jesus Christ in His church.

15

Working for the Lord: The Pay's Not So Good, But You Can't Beat the Retirement Plan

For most of us, having money for our and others' needs requires that we spend much of our time working. We know work ennobles human nature, but we've never really cared much for nobility. If hard work is the key to success, we'd rather pick the lock.

One important part of our personalities is talent. The skills and abilities the Lord has given us are our means of helping others, improving ourselves, and carrying out God's will for our lives. They are also our means of earning the money we have been talking about.

Using those talents, though, takes time. And even then there is always more to do than time to do it. We work from daybreak to backbreak and just keep getting farther behind. We need two trays on our desks; one marked "IN" and the other "IN DEEPER."

Our most sincere attempts to catch up on our work sometimes go for naught. In 1978 an Englishman decided to work through his lunch hour to catch up. Ten minutes after the crew had left for lunch, a cow fell through the roof! Somehow the animal had managed to climb onto the top of the building.

The diligent businessman and the cow stared at each other a short time, and then the animal lowered her head and charged. The man retreated toward the door. Fortunately, the cow stopped to chew a green carpet and the man escaped.

TGIF

You may not be attacked by a cow in your office, but you have other problems. You probably know how it feels to go out to the rat race every day, sure that most of the world is rooting for the rats. After five days a week of that, the only song of praise you can muster is "TGIF": Thank God It's Friday!

The popularity of TGIF is a symptom of the restlessness and dissatisfaction of our working society. We need to restore some of the ecstasy that can be found in working. To acknowledge that man's fall has caused work to become a drudgery does not preclude taking steps to make work more fulfilling and enjoyable. The good news of Scripture is that creation is God's work in which we participate through the activities that provide our livelihood.

No matter what occupation we are engaged in, our work is important. God has a place for our activity and products in His divine plan. Unfortunately, we tend to lose our sense of value when we see our jobs becoming more routine or yielding no tangible results. We get bored. The Underwriters Council of Melbourne, Australia, approved full workmen's compensation for anyone dislocating his jaw while yawning at work.

Everyone of us can contribute substantially to the advancement of the human race through the jobs we do. We need only to dedicate ourselves totally to the work into which the Holy Spirit leads us. Your job may seem dull or insignificant. You may find yourself yearning to accomplish "greater things." And yet if you invest your life serving Christ as a partner with God in His creative process, the value of your work is immeasurable.

Recognizing that the work we do makes us fellow workers with God can bring considerable joy—even to the most cumbersome task. No matter how lowly our jobs may seem, we will be more ready to give them our best effort.

Some time ago a television weather reporter from Philadelphia spoke at a college in North Carolina. He told of feeling unappreciative of his job until he had dinner with a group of senior citizens in New Jersey. The old folks made considerable fuss over the weatherman, and he assumed it was because they had seen his face on TV. But one of the oldtimers corrected him. "We are making a celebrity of you not because you are on television, but because you are the weatherman. At our age, the weatherman is the only fellow who promises us a tomorrow."

Too many of us spend the first two work days of the week recovering from the weekend and the next three planning the weekend. Our priorities should be reversed, from working in order to play, to playing in order to work. A violinist loosens the strings of his instrument at night but tightens them the next day so that he can again produce beautiful music. So also workers loosen their strings at night, enjoying a night out, relaxing at home or engaging in a favorite hobby. So, too, they enjoy a weekend of golf, pro football, or rest. But the goal must be increased readiness to go back to work as a diplomat on assignment from the kingdom of God and perform the tasks required by our jobs.

Choosing a Career

One factor adding to the natural drudgery of our jobs is doing work for which we are not suited. The careers we select are sometimes not those that might make best use of our talents.

When we speak of talents, we are usually referring to the human activities we do best. Some of us are good at repairing heart valves, others at repairing engine valves. Some of us have trouble just putting a washer in a faucet. What we do best is one important consideration in choosing a career. When a client comes to me for vocational counseling, we talk about these abilities and often use an aptitude test to measure them. Sometimes, especially with younger people, talents are uncovered the client has not been aware of.

These special *aptitudes*, though, are just one of three main considerations in career choice. Just as important are *interests* and *values*.

We aren't always interested in the things we do best. I have counseled many young people whose aptitude scores suggested they could successfully pursue any profession they might choose, but who have still been more interested in pursuing a career as a tradesperson. When this discrepancy between ability and interest exists, we tend to shut our minds and wills to our talents and move in the direction of our interests.

This can be an unwise move, since talents or aptitudes are more permanent than interests. Shifting interests can result in regret over abilities unused or undeveloped. A decision not to pursue a career that uses a special talent should be made only with great caution.

Another common stumbling block is pursuing careers we are interested in but have no aptitude for. Like many men, I can remember childhood dreams of being a great athlete. It can be frustrating and sometimes very costly to try to move into a career for which we do not have the required physical or emotional make-up.

A cashier in a Whitesville, Kentucky, bank was too softhearted for the job. When financial instability forced the bank to close, a liquidator from the Federal Deposit Insurance Corporation investigated. He discovered that the bank had accepted more than 2000 worthless checks, totalling $535,000. The fifty-one-year-old cashier admitted that he had honored the checks, ranging from $1 to $7000 over a four-year period. Often he knew the checks were worthless, but he felt like indulging the customer, and he assumed the checks would eventually be made good.

The liquidator also found 135 accounts overdrawn. Two of the overdrafts totalled about $160,000 each. The cashier had covered these shortages by hiding good accounts from the bank examiners and using this money to balance the overdrafts.

Values

Of the criteria for choosing a career, none is more important than values, those things we consider important. These provide the motivation for our work and should guide our vocational selection.

According to a recent survey, only one American worker in five believes that income is the most important factor in his job. Half the respondents indicated that the most important thing about a job is its significance and the feeling of accomplishment it yields.

Eighty-four percent of American workers find their jobs meaningful; eighty-one percent say they are interesting; eighty-nine percent feel their work affects many people. Ninety percent of working Americans say they're satisfied with their job, while sixty percent claim they would recommend the job to a friend.

These are encouraging findings, but our work value system must go even deeper. The first justification for any job is the service of God. Our work achieves this if we do our best to perform it faithfully. Work that further contributes to the common good in practical and material ways, or a job in which we give ourselves to the service of others, may be especially worthwhile. Fundamentally though, it is performing a task because God wants us to that justifies whatever work we do.

Not long ago, my son came home from school perplexed. He had struggled with one assignment for a long time and turned in what he felt was a good product. His grade on this paper was a B. For the same course, he had produced a very rapid piece of work on another assignment and received an A.

You've had this kind of thing happen; we all have. We've studied hard for a test and gotten a low grade and taken another with little preparation and done well. We've put considerable effort into one job-related assignment and gotten no recognition for it and then dealt casually with another and received commendation.

These events are reminders that our efforts are not always effective. There is no direct relationship between how hard we try and what kind of results we produce. God controls the results of our activity. He wants us to put as much as we can into each task because in this way we progress in our personal growth toward Him. It is what we put into a task that matters, not what results come from it.

Judging Our Accomplishments

Over and over again, in whatever tasks we undertake, in whatever line of work we do, we need reminders. The fundamental truth is this: What we become, not what we produce, is the really important result of life's work.

Because our viewpoint gets distorted, we often misjudge the real meaning and value of our work. When we compare what we are able to do with the total output of man's efforts or with the great accomplishments of men of history, our contribution seems insignificant. Sometimes we get discouraged because we achieve so little.

A more accurate evaluation of our work would be based on the intensity of our love or the purity of our motives. When we offer our work to Christ, what might otherwise be worthless activity becomes immeasurably worthwhile. Even if your job is as hollow as a drum, you can get a lively rhythm from it. Suddenly the postal clerk has as much dignity as the world's most renowned brain surgeon.

In no way does God need the results of our effort. Instantly, He could erect the world's tallest building as easily as He created the universe around it. What He asks of us is that we invest ourselves in the work He has for us to do with all the dedication and love we are capable of.

In His life on earth, Christ fulfilled perfectly the will of His Father. He was an obedient carpenter's son because this was the Father's will. The person most like Christ is not necessarily the carpenter or the teacher of today. Rather, that man is most like Christ who is faithful to God in his own calling as Christ was faithful in His.

It's possible, then, for any of us to live in close conformity to the likeness of Christ. We need not be a celibate monk or an active minister. The lawyer who is just in practice, the family man or woman, the farmer or the salesman—any of us can carry out God's will for our lives.

This viewpoint brings us a new perspective. It introduces rich meaning into the most humdrum of occupations. It reminds us that our life is not what we make it, but that God chooses our place and sets our task for us. Actress Ginger Rogers once said that she never goes on stage without thinking: "Man is not a worker, he is God's work going on." I like that!

Dedication

A more accurate perspective of why we are working has great potential for increasing the fulfillment our jobs provide. Anyone who thinks money will do everything is likely to do everything for money. But working just to make money is always less satisfying than doing work one enjoys. Anyone who holds a job he really doesn't care about, even if it pays well, is likely to find himself enveloped all day long in boredom, watching the clock, and wondering why the second hand takes so long to go around.

On the other hand, if your job challenges your abilities, and you see it as an opportunity to give yourself in love to God's work, you'll enjoy your work and find in it an important means of personal growth.

Working for the Lord

When I was young, I used to hear people talking about how early farmers had to get up to go to work in their fields. I remember that I used to feel this would be impossible for me. Rising at such an early hour to go to work was something I could not imagine. By the grace of God, I now rise at 3:30 or 4:00 A.M. to begin writing. I know that this is the work the Lord has called me to do. I find it richly rewarding, a means of great personal satisfaction.

There are literally hundreds of careers in which men and women can serve God by helping others and encouraging the spread of Christian beliefs and practices. Teachers, for example, exert a powerful influence. The field of medicine provides the challenge to help others as a doctor, a nurse, a medical technologist or attendant. Social workers help those in the community with problems beyond their own ability to solve. Persons in politics and public service make and enforce the laws necessary for a better society. Communication workers produce newspapers, magazines, television programs, radio broadcasts, and motion pictures; these have a profound effect upon people's attitudes and conduct. An outstanding entertainer or athlete may influence thousands of youngsters who might not respond to any other kind of example or teaching. The person who repairs a television set or automobile, the supermarket worker, the butcher, baker, electrician, plumber or carpenter, the pharmacist, the policeman and fireman who guard the community—all are worthy, respected members of society. While performing their services with dedication, they can know that those they serve are better for having come in contact with them.

What You're Worth

When you feel you'll never get all the work done, remember that you are collaborating in founding Christ's kingdom. Christ mixes His redeeming blood with your daily sweat and works with you to build a world in which love rules.

Christ works with us in our offices as we pore over columns of figures. He is beside us in our factories, surrounded by noise. He is jammed with us into the subway, waiting with us in restaurants, hurrying with us to get to a meeting on time.

Our role in promoting Christ's kingdom is more than just a matter of offering up the jobs we perform to give meaning to work that has no value of its own. Christ is at work in the smallest particle of matter, and His creative action unites with ours in every kind of work we do.

Nearly every father has had the experience of receiving a gift from a child that has no value beyond what paternal love might attach to it. We often think of God as receiving our work in much the same way as a father reacts to such a gift. Truly, it is "the thought that counts." But as we seek to unite our efforts with Christ's, we come closer to bringing our father an ashtray he can really use, a tie that complements his favorite suit, a tool he will need to do a job planned for the weekend.

In Ecclesiastes we are reminded of the futility of our efforts when we do not work for the Lord: "Vanity of vanities, says Qoheleth, vanity of vanities! All things are vanity! What profit has man from all the labor which he toils at under the sun?" (1:2,3). When we do the Lord's work, no human standard can reflect the worth of our labor.

Your Paycheck

No matter what you think your contribution is worth, you might sometimes have to push for a higher salary. Even with the cost of living and seniority raises that are standard practice in many businesses and professions, a strategy when asking for an increase doesn't hurt. Let me set down a four-point plan that might be useful when you find yourself in this situation.

1. Make a judgment about your value to the company or profession. Compare the quality and quantity of your work with that of your coworkers. Do you have more responsibility, do you accomplish more, do you spend more time on the job?

2. List your traits and talents that contribute most to the job. What have your major contributions been in the past year? What special projects have you been given responsibility for?

3. Submit your request early in the budget development period. You'll have to know when your boss prepares departmental budgets. Timing your request is extremely important because a "we'll see" is seldom more than a polite refusal.

4. Plan carefully what you will say in submitting your request. Limit your time to three to four minutes, and try to take advantage of one of your boss's more pleasant moods. Anticipate his objections; have arguments ready to reinforce your request. On the other hand, don't apply pressure or try to back your boss into a corner. Give him time to digest what you say and to give you an answer when he is ready.

16

It's Easier for a Rich Man to Enter Heaven Than for a Poor Man to Remain on Earth

Chewing on a toothpick, I was sitting and reading the *Book of Lists*. Near the end of the volume, I came to the heading "25 Deaths from Strange Causes." The second entry on this list is that of Agathocles, who lived in Syracuse around 300 B.C. Agathocles reportedly met his death by choking on a toothpick. After I had dropped the stick I was chewing on into the garbage can, I read on. In 1478, George, Duke of Clarence, is reported to have died when his brother Richard the Third had him drowned in a barrel of wine.

Thomas Otway, a seventeenth-century English dramatist, went without food for days and started to beg. Someone gave Otway a guinea, which he used to buy a roll. He choked to death on the first mouthful.

Arnold Bennett, British novelist, wanted to demonstrate that the water in Paris was safe to drink. He drank a glassful, contracted typhoid, and died.

Well, we all get to go sometime. Some of us first have to live many years for the Lord to bring us where he wants us. Gradually, we feel the sediment clogging the pipes of our fountain of youth. We stop being bothered by insurance salesmen and find that even our hot flashes are lukewarm. Then one morning we wake up with nothing hurting, and we're sure we're dead.

But no, not yet.

Delays

Stories of people mistakenly proclaimed dead can be found in any culture. In the late 1800s a funeral was held in Delhi for an oriental missionary named Dr. Schwartz. At the end of the ceremony, the congregation intoned the missionary's favorite hymn. During the final verse, the mourners were amazed to hear a voice from the coffin joining in!

Many sports figures have gained recognition by making amazing comebacks. But there never was another comeback quite like that of jockey Ralph Neves. At Bay Meadows in 1936 Neves' horse tripped as he entered the stretch, flinging the jockey headfirst into the rail. The track doctor examined Neves and announced that his heart had stopped beating. In a desperate attempt to save him, an ambulance rushed the jockey to the hospital, but revival efforts were futile. Pronounced dead, he was covered with a sheet.

"I knew I didn't feel dead," Neves said later, "even if I was sore all over."

When Neves spoke to the doctor, the physician got "as white as the sheet he had covered me with." Neves went on to report, "I was rushed to a hospital bed, which seemed silly to me when I knew I was billed to ride Instigator in the seventh race."

Left alone in his room, Neves got dressed, sneaked out, and returned to the track in a cab. Neves' fellow jockeys were shocked when he walked into the jockeys' quarters at the precise moment they were taking up a collection for his funeral. The jockey's wife was just returning from a tearful meeting of condolences from the track president. She fainted.

Neves suited up for the seventh race and went on to become one of the country's top jockeys.

The thought of hearing yourself pronounced dead is a bit eerie, isn't it? In recent years several prominent doctors—most notably Dr. Elisabeth Kübler-Ross—have carefully

197

studied persons in the process of dying. In a number of cases, those who had been declared clinically dead were subsequently revived, and they described what they had experienced. Their stories contain a number of common elements. Most of these patients reported looking down on their lifeless bodies and watching the doctors work on them. Most experienced a sensation of moving through a long tunnel toward a door or gate that represented the point of no return. A warm glow proceeded from an extremely bright source of light.

We'll all, someday, go through that tunnel toward the Source. If we've lived well, we won't worry about taking our possessions with us. Happily we lay it all down to ". . . inherit the kingdom prepared for you from the creation of the world" (Matt. 25:34).

Anticipating Heaven

What will heaven be like?

Christ has told us most emphatically that our human minds cannot progress beyond the foggiest notion of heaven. With this fact established, though, we are given many glimpses of insight into what heaven will be like. God knows that our limited faith needs the reinforcement of understanding.

Christ Himself has provided some comparisons for us: "In my Father's house are many mansions," or "The kingdom of heaven is like a mustard seed." It is important to realize that each of these is, in fact, nothing more than a comparison designed to increase our appreciation. Dealing with concrete realities that can be grasped by our human intelligence, they don't really begin to scratch the surface of God's infinity.

A child, hearing that sexual enjoyment was the highest form of bodily pleasure, asked, "Do you eat chocolate while you're doing it?" We often react in much the same way when we hear about the perfect happiness of heaven. Our notion of happiness is formed by our experiences. We have known the joy of loving sexual fulfillment. We have shared the delight of embracing a child we have begotten. We have tasted delectable meals. We have known the passing delight of riches or prestige.

We have not gazed in rapturous adoration upon the unimaginable beauty of God Himself. But we do know that the very best of all earthly delights will be perfected in the beatific vision that is our eternal reward. Gladly, we will lay our Hershey bar aside and enter into perfect joy.

A man and his nine-year-old daughter were touring Washington and passed the National Archives Building. The youngster read the inscription engraved on the front of the building, a quotation from Shakespeare's *Tempest:* "What is past is prologue." She asked her father, "Daddy, what does that mean?"

"It means," the father replied, "you ain't seen nothin' yet!"

The past *is* prologue. Everything that has occurred in our lives—yes, everything in the temporal realm—is prologue to the eternity we will share with our Creator. And, as Christ has assured us, the best is yet to come. Not only has eye not seen, but ear has not heard, nor has it entered into the human heart to imagine the wonders prepared for us.

Till It's Time to Go

All right. We can't take it with us. Still, we'd like to have it last until we're ready to go. And with the rising cost of funerals we might not even be able to afford to go. Cemeteries keep raising the price of burial plots, blaming it all on the cost of living.

We do have to go on living from day to day, but the thought of death can be a valuable means of staying on the right path. Most of us have acquaintances diagnosed as terminally ill. With such a prospect before me, what would I do differently? If the best medical opinion available indicated that I had seven days of life left, how would I spend them?

I remember that someone once replied to a similar inquiry by saying he would not change anything. He would simply go on performing the duties of his state of life as well as he could, knowing that this was God's will for him. If I could honestly give a similar response, I would feel much more secure about the kind of eternity my life-style has shaped for me.

No, there are some things I would have to change. Maybe the easiest would be becoming detached from material things. I'd stop complaining so much and become more aware of the many blessings I've had in my life. I'd talk more of richness and less of deprivation. I'd harbor less resentment toward people who reject or belittle me, and I'd be much more eager to love others and accept them as they are.

Above all, my eagerness to love would come forth in my family relationships. A new sense of urgency would help me make up for violations of that love: lust, harsh words, impatience, indifference.

Many things in our lives besides the immediate threat of death can help us remember our eternal destiny. Cut flowers, for example. A bouquet of spring blossoms, daisies and daffodils, carnations and mums, can be as beautiful as the most colorful garden. They're dead, though, cut off from their roots and their soul. Soon they will begin to wilt and, in a few days, go into a bag with the old coffee grounds, empty cans, and potato peels. They'll be hauled off in the weekly trash collection.

When we sin, we short-circuit ourselves from our source of life. Through deliberate choice of evil, we damage the stem and block the channel of spiritual life to our souls. Viewed from outside, we may look attractive for a while. All too soon, though, time serves God's purpose and wilting begins.

Entering the Kingdom

"Do Not Enter." To encounter this sign at the gates of heaven is the most frightening prospect I can imagine. We know that to lose our eternal happiness is to frustrate the very purpose for which we have been created. And yet the

Lord has told us in no uncertain terms that unless we become "as little children" we *shall not* enter there. We must return to the childlike simplicity that frees us to lay all our complex interests in the hands of our Father and focus only on His love.

How can we do this?

If we would only let God show us! Again and again He beckons to us, offering to lead us to simple love. But despite the words we mouth, we would rather be led into temptation.

He'll stay with it. Of this we can be sure. We have countless examples in biblical history of how God leads man to his limit so that man can be free. He led Abraham to the limit of trust when he promised that a barren Sarah would be fruitful. He led Moses to the impassability of the Red Sea. Sarah bore a son. The waters of the Red Sea parted!

Help me realize, Lord, that emptiness must come before filling. Help me to be more aware that only as my spirit is stripped of the things it craves can it be filled to abundance with Your richness.

Before anyone of us can pass through heaven's portals we must lay down the cost of admission. Oh, none of us could ever pay the full price. Christ's death, though, has given everyone of us safe passage. All we need to "pay" is all we are and all we have.

That's not much, really. Not in relation to the inheritance that is ours as children of God. Not in relation to the eternal gift of God Himself in the pure union of our heavenly home.

This pure union, this relationship with God the Father, God the Son, and God the Holy Spirit cannot be ours as long as we retain our attachments to earthly possessions. We must give them up—completely.

God and Money

We all need to seek detachment from the world. It's a mistake, though, to think of this detachment as lack of caring or as passivity. We can remain committed to serving the world and yet grow in our freedom from *selfish* attachment. In fact, only as we decrease the extent of our selfishness can we really serve others. Only as we get rid of the blindness that comes with self-service can we see things as they really are and use them as they are intended to be used.

We are often blind to the needs of others because we are too engrossed in our own needs. We become too concerned with providing for ourselves and our family. It *is* our duty to take care of ourselves and those dependent on us, but once we have assured the provision of minimal needs for the present, we should begin to look beyond our own homes to recognize the urgent needs of our fellow human beings.

Instead, we worry about the future. Sure we have enough bread on the table now, but what if there is a depression? Or, how will we take care of the expenses that come with educating our children?

I wish I could convince you, dear reader, that the best way to provide for tomorrow is to give generously of today's surplus to those who need it. If you try to hold on to what you have as a protection against the heavy financial demands of a vague future, you'll find thieves, moths, and rust will consume what you have. Trust in the Lord and share willingly, and He will provide for all your future needs.

In the story of the rich man and his unjust steward, Jesus surprised his disciples with an Edgar Allen Poe-type ending. The steward had dissipated his master's resources and was being fired from his job. He decided as a last act of his stewardship to gain himself some friends. One after another he called in his master's debtors and decreased the amount of their obligations. The surprise is that when the owner learned of what his devious employee was doing, he gave him credit for being enterprising!

After concluding this story, Christ went on to encourage his disciples to make friends for themselves through the use of this world's goods. But he was talking about true friends, the kind that provide "a lasting reception." For Jesus went on to say, "If you can trust a man in little things, you can also trust him in greater; while anyone unjust in a slight matter is also unjust in greater. If you can not be trusted with elusive wealth, who will trust you with lasting? And if you have not been trustworthy with someone else's money, who will give you what is your own? No servant can serve two masters. Either he will hate the one and love the other, or he will be attentive to the one and despise the other. You can not give yourself to God and money" (Luke 16:10–13).

Hasn't the Lord given us abundant evidence of His loving care? He fed 5000 people with less food than you're allowed in that new diet your corpulent doctor prescribed. Throughout our lives He has shown us his generosity and loving care. No matter how dark the night or how far we wander from home, we know that in His care we are totally secure.